All's Fair in Love & Karma

5 Steps to Relationship Mastery

June Edward

Psychic Medium, Event Speaker,
Teacher, Author, Relationship Expert

Al's Fair in Love & Karma

5 Steps to Relationship Mastery

ISBN: 9798866392155

Independently published

Printed in the United States of America

All's Fair in Love & Karma

5 Steps to Relationship Mastery

This book is dedicated to all the angels, guides, and loved ones on the other side. They have been my greatest teachers in this lifetime. I will be forever grateful and humbled by their wisdom and knowledge. — June Edward

Contents

Foreword

Love lessons, or lessons in love, are all one and the same. Can someone die of a broken heart? I believe they can. In previous decades, a number of husbands and/or wives have died within minutes or hours after losing their life partner. Everyone wants to love and be loved; love is something that ties us all together as a common quest in life. People have killed for love; many were willing to die for love or to take someone else's place to die for love. Some of the most important decisions in our life are made for love or come from loving another person. People have sacrificed and suffered in the name of love and even killed themselves out of a displaced notion of love.

Love is the highest vibration of energy we can have, and it is the strongest motivator known to mankind. Why is it that so many people find love not only to be elusive but difficult to understand? Some think love is some magic potion or a combination of something magical that they think they are missing. Some people are never sure if they truly love someone, or if love is an infatuation that wears off all too soon.

To understand our five-love lessons is to know and understand what true love is and why we decide to love someone specific—or to love no one at all. There is no one-size-fits-all answer because everyone has a different life journey. The only thing that ties us all together is the five love lessons that we all need to learn. At the end of our lives, the only two things we take with us are love and knowledge. Hence, there are five love lessons that we all need to learn. They survive from lifetime to lifetime and teach us what true love is and what our journeys are all about.

Love is a connection of the soul, not just of the body. It is a fine mix of caring, empathy, chemistry, and a little delusion. The reason a relationship lasts as long as it does is that we fall in love with the same person over and over again. When we are "in love," we overlook faults and decide to just accept them, because the deep soul love that we feel is the "magic" that appears when we are learning our love lessons.

Believe that you can have whatever you want in this lifetime and it will not be difficult. When you learn how to work with your soul, with the angels and the Universe, love, and everything else you want comes to you. Use this book as a reference; read it as many times as you need to so you fully understand what it is you need from it. Read it with an open mind and an open heart.

Our Reincarnations

As souls, we reincarnate many times on this earth, into many different bodies. We all come here for basically the same reasons. We come to Earth in a body to play, to help others, and for our soul to continue its growth by learning our five love lessons. They are the basis for the highest growth our soul can attain. We learn much faster on this side than on the other side, even though in the grand scheme of things, we are only here for a very short time.

We start to forget all the knowledge and wisdom we previously had and the reasons we came here as we grow from a baby to a small child. Did you ever notice how happy a baby is? How a baby smiles and laughs and reaches out like it sees things that you do not? That is because they *still do* see things. Their soul is still fresh from the other side, and they still see and converse on a soul level with the angels and souls that are all around them. Many children continue to see entities from the other side until they start being told that it is their imagination. It is really a normal state but we have been conditioned to believe otherwise. There have been many documented cases of young children who still remember their last lifetime and can give detailed information as to who they were, where they lived, to whom they were married, etc.

A very famous psychic, Chip Coffey, had one of the first paranormal television shows, specifically on this topic. If you cannot find him in reruns, Chip Coffey has some very interesting YouTube videos for skeptics to watch. He was one of the first psychics to have his own television show focused solely on the children that remembered their past lives.

Even though we are all born with psychic abilities, our bodies are poisoned over time and our penial glands calcified from fluoride in our water supplies to hinder the development of psychic abilities amongst the population. Our penial gland is a small walnut-sized gland in the middle of our forehead. It has been proven to be made of the same cells that our eyeballs are made from. Amazingly, our ancestors knew this, hence the reason it has been dubbed "the third eye." It is filled with a clear fluid that acts like a reflecting pool. Images are sent energetically from the other side, as well as telepathically from souls on this side, and our souls are able to translate the images reflected in the penial gland into messages.

In order to stop people from receiving these messages, the government has added fluoride to our drinking water. It calcifies the fluid in the pineal gland and stops us from receiving these image messages. Fluoride is a byproduct of aluminum and iron ore and is a known poison. Excess amounts can also cause other physical problems such as osteoporosis, arthritis, and muscular damage, among other things.

In order to truly learn your five love lessons, you have to learn how to get in touch with and access your soul— the real you. Anything that can be done to stop you from accessing your soul and psychic abilities will be done so that you can be controlled easier by the government and the evil powers that are in charge.

Through the last few centuries, there has been a campaign to stigmatize people who openly acknow-ledge their psychic abilities and are in touch with both their souls and the other side. Some were branded as witches—not just in the Americas, but in other countries as well—and were killed. A thousand years ago, those people who mastered their abilities were advisors to the rulers, known as the Maji. These physics were revered, and everyone was encouraged to listen to their souls and their psychic abilities. As time went on, the rulers began to fear people who had developed these psychic abilities, and in order to control them, they tried to make these abilities illegal, claiming they were dangerous.

Today, many people with expanded psychic abilities are told they are freaks, liars, and cheats. This is not to say that everyone in the physic field is honest; it is the same as in any other profession. There are good doctors and lousy doctors. There are good lawyers and others that are not so good. Many people are taught to not trust mediums and psychics, to fear them, and are not encouraged to enhance their own abilities. Children that have extraordinary abilities, or still see souls from the other side, are put off as playful, daydreamers, or just fantasizing. Their parents and teachers tell them it is not real, and to ignore what they see and feel. Eventually, they do, if only because they do not want to feel stigmatized, as I did when I was a child. I have found that when you tell people what is going to happen, and it does, they label you as a freak.

Angels exist, your friends and loved ones who have passed to the other side still exist, they just do not have a body anymore. We are all pure energy, and energy cannot be destroyed or created, only changed. I always find it interesting, that when on their deathbeds, there are very few atheists. The closer you get to returning to the other side, the more you are willing to consider the possibilities that you cannot necessarily see. The closer you get to death, the thinner the veil between the two worlds becomes, and the more you catch "glimpses" of the souls and angels here visiting you.

My own father was very skeptical about my abilities until he was about a year from passing due to advanced prostate and bladder cancer. (I came out of the closet, so to speak, as a psychic medium at the age of fifty-two.) One day when I was visiting him, he said that he wanted to talk to me about what I do and what I see.

"Really? What's changed your mind?"

He went on to tell me that every time he falls asleep and wakes up, he sees his mother standing next to his bed. He said it had been happening for months. I laughed a little and told him that it was about time. I let him know that I had seen her there every time I came to visit him and that he was probably seeing her when he first awoke until his mind blocked it out in disbelief. She had been watching over him, I explained, and she was waiting to escort him to the other side when it was time for him to go.

I went on to describe the angels that had been around him as well and told him what he could expect when he gets to the other side. He seemed very grateful for the information, and his mind seemed to be put to rest. Just as interesting, since he has passed, another medium brought him through and I saw him around me. My father was saying he enjoyed playing golf, which he liked but never did while here, and fishing, which he had not done since he was a boy but had always wanted to do. He visits me occasionally but keeps it brief. I understand he came here for certain lessons; however, he is not my favorite soul to have a visit with.

I have had the honor of seeing a few souls actually leave their bodies at the time of their death, including my mother's. It literally looks like moving air, or like mist rising from their head. If they go into the light, they come back with an immeasurable amount of energy. If they stay stuck here, and become what most people call "ghosts," their energy is the same as it was when they were alive—lower vibrational. They are not able to move about at lightning speed. In fact, they cannot move any faster than you or I. In this book, I will teach you some of what I have learned since I came back from the other side, and how it all ties into the love lessons you came here to learn.

Some of us are older souls and have much to teach others. Not to say we are not all still learning—we are—but if we understand how to tap into the wisdom we brought with us from previous lifetimes, we can offer so much more to help others.

Most of us have reincarnated, at a minimum, many hundreds of times. We have come here to enjoy what we cannot when our soul is on the other side and bodyless. Without a body, you cannot taste, smell, touch, have sex, or experience other things that you need a body for. Souls that are still on the other side have to live vicariously through us. That is why it has been said to set another plate at the dinner table, and they will join you. If you are enjoying a meal, they will come to enjoy it with and through you. They love being remembered, and since they are still fairly new to the other side, they want to be remembered. If you are sad, however, they will stay by your side and be sad with you instead of enjoying themselves on the other side and attending to the learning we still do there.

We also do not miraculously turn into someone else when we die. If the person was a jerk or a mean person when they were here, they are still a jerk or a mean person on the other side. It takes a long time for a soul to heal and change unless they want to.

My own sister, who passed away many years ago, hated me when she was alive. She had a mental illness, and I had been her legal guardian for a good part of her life. After she had been on the other side for about one year of their time and three of our years, she came to me and apologized. She explained how she had been very jealous of me when she was alive and resented me for having control over her life. She told me she had been through therapy with the angels on the other side and now understood how she had been acting and treating people while she was here. She wanted to understand because she did not want to have to live such a challenging life the next time she was reincarnated.

The best way to explain contact from those on the other side is to imagine a two-way mirror. You only see yourself, but they are banging on it trying to get your attention. They can see you, hear you, and some can even learn how to use their energy to touch you and move objects.

I have two students who converse with their loved ones through a yes-and-no system with lights, and another, whose fiancé had passed away, sends messages through his cellphone. You, however, for the most part, cannot see or hear them unless you are in touch with your soul and paying attention. It is all very frustrating for them; all they want is to help you if they can, to guide you on your path here, and help you to learn your love lessons. All you need to do is think of them, and they are right there with you. It does not matter where they are in the Universe, they will show up when asked. You can learn to increase your psychic ability to see and hear them if you so choose. I will teach you how to do that later in the book.

What about the love lessons that we came here to learn? We chose the lessons we still need to learn prior to coming here, and eventually, we have to learn all the love lessons to complete our soul growth. We literally decide who will be in our life to teach us and who we are here to help. We choose our parents, our children, and even who we will love and interact with. It is like designing your own board game. If you owe karma to someone from a past lifetime, or they owe you, they will be written into your life plan. Some people even choose to build in an "out" if they feel that the plan they made is too intense, and they may need to leave this earth early.

Apparently, I did, because I literally died at the age of twenty-seven and came back here by choice. That is correct, I died; I have been to the other side, and I came back. I will give you a little more information on how that all transpired in an upcoming chapter. The only unacceptable "out" is suicide. If you commit suicide, you have basically quit the game of life, and the angels have to scramble to correct every situation and person you were supposed to interact with while you were supposed to be here.

It is very true that you have no idea how many lives one person can affect and change. We are the most powerful beings, each and every one of us. Most souls that commit suicide regret it once they get to the other side because they realize how many people they have let down and hurt. They have to go through more intense "therapy" on the other side before being allowed to reincarnate so that they do not leave early again.

What Are Our Love Lessons?

The greatest lessons in life are taught in our closest relationships, whether that be a romantic relationship or a relationship with family or friends. It is one of the main reasons that we come here to Earth—also to have some fun from living with a body. There are lots of things that we learn through life, but there are five major love lessons we all come here to learn within our relationships. Many of the lessons are intertwined with each other and tied to another lesson. Many lessons are reinforced over and over through the intertwining of the lessons. Everyone needs to eventually learn all five of the love lessons so that their soul can advance. Some lessons you may believe you already know, and that may be the lesson that leads you right into the next lesson that you need to learn. I will go into depth on each of the love lessons, but the following is an outline of what they are.

Self-worth

Understanding your importance and that you need to put yourself first

Without your health and well-being, you will not be able to help others. It is not narcissistic or selfish to put yourself first; it is where everything else comes from. We are not here to be sacrificial martyrs and put everyone else first.

Money-Balance

Learning how money works and what it represents

Money is another form of energy; hence, the reason it is called currency. It needs to flow like a river in order for it to work properly and have it come back to you even stronger. The whole Universe needs to stay in balance, and people need to maintain balance in every area of their lives. Without balance, we struggle to maintain everything.

Trust and Communication

We have to learn to trust a higher power

Whatever you want to name this power, there is only one. We have to trust that everything happens for a reason; there are no coincidences and things are always going to work out for our highest and best result. We have to learn how to get in touch with—and trust—our own souls. People also have to learn to communicate their wants, needs, and desires. Most people are not adept at reading minds. If you do not communicate your needs, they will not be fulfilled. If you do not let others know what they mean to you, they will not know. Sex with another person is just another form of communication. It requires trust outside the bedroom first.

Unconditional love

Learning that people are not doing things "to you" or to "hurt you"

They are doing what they are supposed to do to learn their own lessons. Everything is not always about you but may be about someone else's lesson in life. The answer to every question is love; it is a very disarming answer. You can love someone and not really like them: these are really two different things. You can also love them and not have them in your life. You can always send love; it is the highest form of energy, and it is how you raise your vibration the fastest, as well as how you show that you are being grateful.

Patience

Everything comes in the time that it is supposed to— whatever is in your life plan

You cannot rush the things in your life or push them to happen. We only recognize time here on Earth; the rest of the Universe has no recognition of "time." Some souls have been around for hundreds of thousands of years, continually reincarnating. Your higher self, the part of your soul in the lowest level of heaven, orchestrates the timing of all the events in your life, following the plan that you laid out before coming here. Patience is not waiting; it is the knowledge that the things you want to happen will happen while you live your life and go about your daily business. You trust and know that the Universe will implement your plan.

How Do I Know What I Know?

I will take a moment and explain to you how I know about the things that I am about to impart to you. I was born with what is considered to be an excess of psychic abilities, abilities that everyone has. Everyone is born with psychic abilities and mediumship abilities. Some people have more natural abilities than others because it is their life path, but everyone possesses these abilities. How quickly you learn your five love lessons is all a matter of how much you choose to pay attention to your own abilities and get in touch with your soul. Thousands of years ago, it was not only acceptable but children were also taught how to listen to their "guts," or psychic abilities, to keep them out of danger in life. Mental telepathy was a common occurrence since thoughts are things. Where your thoughts go, your energy flows. If you're thinking about someone, the odds are pretty high that they are also thinking about you.

When I was a small child, I would see people standing around my bed at night and waking me up in the morning. I would see faces staring at me from behind my curtains across the room. I would hear them calling my name and think it was my parents.

I would get out of bed, go to their bedroom, and find my parents fast asleep. I would go back to bed and pull the covers up over my head, only to see the shadows of them above me if I opened my eyes. I could see people and hear some of them talking to me throughout the day. I did not even question if other people saw them or not; I just assumed that they did.

As a child, I learned that other people did not see them, and it was a frightening experience. I was also very psychic and thought I was just experiencing what people call déjà vu. I would go somewhere new to me and feel like I had already been there before. I would know things were going to happen before they actually did.

Going to school and telling the other children what was going to happen before it happened was also an innocent mistake, but it quickly got me labeled as a freak, and I was bullied verbally for it. For this reason, I tried very hard to block my abilities and became very shy and standoffish toward other people. I even developed a stutter as a child because I could not get my thoughts out fast enough; I was fighting the nervousness I felt being around other people.

When I was ten years old, my parents separated, and my dad kidnapped the youngest five of eight children, including me. We moved into a house that was closer to his business, about an hour away from where we had been living. I never liked to go into the basement of the house, even if I was with someone else. I could see people in the shadows and the corners of the basement, and it always felt very cold to me, even in the heat of summer.

My household chore as a child of ten was to wash the dishes after supper every night. There was a woman who would come into the kitchen every night and talk to me on a regular basis to keep me company while I stood at the sink and did the dishes. I actually enjoyed her company since I found dishwashing to be a boring chore. I told my older brother about her one morning and asked who she was. I just assumed he must have seen her as well. He laughed and told me that she was the ghost of the woman who used to live in the house. He said her drunken husband had murdered her in the house by throwing her down the basement stairs. That scared me so much that I was afraid of her. She must have sensed it as well because she never came back again.

For most of my adult life, I continued to try to block the souls that kept trying to get in touch with me. However, when someone passed away, even if they were just someone I barely knew but my family had known them, they would come to visit me after their death. The next day after their visit, I would let my family know that they had passed away. They would think I was kidding until they found out about the death in another way. I was always right.

During my youth, I thought that I would never live to be very old. In fact, I thought I would not live to be the age of thirty. The "knowing" that I had was my soul just giving me a heads-up. Sure enough, I died at the age of twenty-seven. I injured my back in a fall at the age of twenty-two, not long after I had gotten married. I put off having surgery on my lower back to repair a disc for five years because I just knew that I was going to die. My friends, my husband, and my family would tell me that I was just nervous because I was afraid of the surgery, and that I had nothing to worry about. I put the surgery off as long as I could and was told I could not have any more children without the surgery because it would be too dangerous.

The night before the surgery. I was given an MRI test, which included an IV with an iodine-based dye. I explained that I thought I was allergic to the dye because I had it once in the past and had a severe reaction to it. They ignored what I had to say, explained it away, told me it was a normal reaction, and continued on with the test.

As soon as I had been injected with the dye, I coded, and my soul immediately left my body. I went into what is known as the fifth dimension, the lowest level of heaven. I could still visualize everything happening below and beyond. I could see the nurses in the hallways talking about what was happening. I could see nurses and the doctor in the room with the crash cart, using the paddles, injecting the IV line, and not having a lot of luck.

The doctor was starting to panic and tipped the bed completely up to get the blood to rush to my head. I could see him slapping me across the face, and saying that he could not lose me, although I felt none of it. I was not in my body to feel it. I could see and hear everything happening in all areas of the hospital all at once. I was also watching my life passing before my eyes like a movie—all the people who had been important to me and the times that were cherished memories. My children being born, my friends that were very important to me, and the times that I remembered as being very special. Any occasion that brought me great joy was being played out in front of me.

As I was watching all of my life events, and these actions unfolding below me, I started having a conversation with someone from the other side who was standing behind me. I did not turn around to see who it was, because I was still watching the movie of my life. They began telling me that it was not really my time to go, that I could stay if I wanted to; it was my decision. I have since been told that was an "out" that I had written into my life plan that I could have taken if I wanted to. Sometimes we write a life plan that is extremely challenging, and if it gets too intense, we can go back early.

It was amazing on the other side. It was peaceful, with no worries, no weight upon you, and no sadness. I felt love all around me, throughout me, and I felt safe. The only things that I noticed I did take with me were my knowledge, and more so, my wisdom, and the love that I had for everything and everyone. Everything was just bathed in pure light and love. It was honestly the most amazing feeling I have ever had, and I can only re-create it through deep meditation. Many people who return from the other side become depressed and suicidal because they cannot get that being-on-the-other-side feeling back.

The ultimate reason that I came back was for the two children that I had at the time. I knew they were one of the primary reasons I had come here, and I wanted to still experience teaching them and raising them. As soon as I made the decision to return, I was immediately put back into my body. Had I not returned, I would not have had my third son. When I went back and opened my eyes, the doctor was relieved. He told me how lucky I was that this was the end of his month on this testing, and not the beginning. He went on to explain that he was a resident, and had it been the beginning of his month he would have lost me because he probably would not have had the experience to recognize the problem to save me quickly enough. I did not bother telling him it was really my choice, not his.

Years later, when I was having an extraordinarily difficult time in my life, I went to see a Reiki practitioner for some relaxation. Reiki is energy work, and it entails fixing the energy flow throughout your body and aligning the chakras. I have since become not only a Reiki Master in Western Reiki but an Okuden-level Reiki practitioner in the original method of Japanese Reiki.

I was having a very hard time going through a divorce, and I was making decisions in my business and life out of desperation, even though they did not feel right in my "gut." I have since learned that gut feeling is really my soul indicator.

The Reiki practitioner recommended that I try to meditate to relax. At the time, I was running several businesses and did not believe that I could shut my brain down long enough to be able to meditate. The first time that I tried, however, all of my abilities came back a thousand times stronger than when I was a child. I immediately started having experiences where I knew everything about everyone that I was in close proximity to.

I was working at the time doing medical esthetic services in my own business, and everyone I put my hands on was giving me overwhelming psychic messages. All of the clients I saw, after the first day that I had meditated, were first-time clients of the spa. I was taking them as overflow because I was short of technicians, so I did not know them at all.

The first woman I saw, about halfway through her service, I got the overwhelming feeling that her aunt had just died, so I asked her. She confirmed that she had and said she had just finished cleaning out her aunt's house.

"I know it sounds a little crazy," I said, "but did you find a sock puppet in the attic of the house?"

Sock puppets were made in the 1950s, and they looked like a monkey. They were very popular when I was a child. She said that she did and asked me how I knew this. I told her that I really had no idea how I knew, it was just something that came to me. I thought at the time that both of us must have been wondering which one of us was pulling a joke on the other!

This psychic knowledge continued throughout the day. The next client that I had, I got an overwhelming feeling that she was worried about her husband. I asked her if she was worried about him for some reason. She confirmed that she was, and she said it was the first time he had traveled to Florida by himself and she was concerned for his safety. I explained that I was starting to have some type of weird psychic experience that had been happening all day, and I did not know how to stop it. I told her that I was getting messages that her husband was fine, but I kept seeing a small "A" frame blue house on the water, and I asked if it was their house.

She said that she did not recognize the house, that they lived in a big yellow house, nowhere near the water.

We had finished with the appointment, but before she left, she came back into the room to show me the text message she had received from her husband. It had come through while she was having her services with me. It was the picture of the blue house on the water that I had described, with the caption "our new house." It was a house that he saw in Florida and thought she would like. We both could not believe it. Seriously, what are the odds of this happening?

The next woman came in for her facial services, and again, I explained that I was having some strange psychic experiences happening that I couldn't seem to stop and asked her if she wanted me to give her any information if I received anything concerning her. She said sure, that she would be interested.

Even before my training, I knew it would not be ethical to give someone information unless they wanted to receive it. I could possibly give them some information that could potentially change something in their life. I was able to describe her entire home to her, where her Christmas tree was placed as if I was standing in her living room, and what her daughter looked like. I was even able to describe what she had gotten her husband for Christmas. She believed that I must have somehow been to her house, although I assured her that I had not.

If it had been only one person that I had these experiences with that day, I would have thought they were just going along with me, but this was way too much for it to be random.

By the time the next person came in, a young girl, I had a full-fledged apparition standing next to me during the entire service, a very handsome young man in a military uniform. Apparently, the young girl was a widow, and this had been her husband. She did not want to know any information, and I respected that. All I could do was apologize to the soul standing next to me and try to keep my composure while I did her facial service. Needless to say, by this time, I was a bit freaked out. This experience was similar to those I had had when I was a child, but it carried a much stronger sensation and revelation. I searched for someone to help me learn how to control what was happening since I knew—just like when I was a child—that I would not be able to turn it off or control it.

I have heard the saying, "When the student is ready, the teacher will arrive." With that in mind, I began to go through a spiritual magazine that I found, calling everyone that advertised as a psychic. I was getting disappointed because no one knew whom I could contact to learn how to turn off what was happening to me.

Eventually, I was guided to some wonderful people who could help me turn my abilities on and off, like a light switch. People who have experienced what I was going through and who are not as lucky as I was, usually think they are going crazy and try to control it with drugs or alcohol.

I spent several years in training in order to control my abilities and understand who it is that I am conversing with on the other side. One thing led to another, and over time, I was taught a great deal from the other side. I now have the ability to go back and forth to the fifth dimension at will and can read people's Akashic[1] records, also known as their book of life, which are kept in the fifth dimension as well. All the souls, guides, angels and archangels, and other higher vibrational entities have worked with me. I did not believe any of it was real prior to dying that day during my surgery. I always had a hard time with abstract concepts. I was one of the biggest skeptics of the paranormal for sure!

For years I felt connected but afraid of my abilities. When I went on vacations with my family to haunted places, I would sense things, and catch apparitions, especially on camera. But they knew I was not ready to fully embrace my gifts. To be honest, I still had a fear of the unknown, which is something you cannot have if you are going to work with the other side.

After my abilities fully opened up, I worked with several paranormal groups throughout the U.S., Canada, and the U.K. I have been a consultant for several books, and I have helped people remove

---

[1] Akashic records are a compendium of all universal events, thoughts, words, emotions, and intent ever to have occurred in the past, present, or future in terms of all entities and life forms, not just human. The Akashic field consists of a subtle sea of fluctuating energies from which all things arise: atoms and galaxies, stars, and planets, living beings, and even consciousness. This zero-point Akashic Field is the constant and enduring memory of the Universe.
https://en.wikipedia.org/wiki/Akashic_records#:~:text=In%20the%20r eligion%20of%20theosophy,life%20forms%2C%20not%20just%20hum an.

demonic entities from their homes. I have worked on missing person cases in connection with the police departments and helped get information on a murder case. My education took many interesting twists and turns. I was able to understand how dangerous evil is and that it is definitely at work in our world.

It is always very important for everyone to have religious pictures, statues, crosses, etc., both in their home and on their person. I do not adhere to any one religion; I believe that they are all right and that they are all wrong, but they all serve a purpose.

Evil entities and the souls that are stuck here will not usually bother you if they see you believe in a higher power. It is too easy for them to go after another soul that does not believe in a higher power and will not put up a fight. They ultimately want to take over your body since they do not have one. The soul's that are stuck here cannot move any faster than you or me and like to hitchhike in cars to get around, so I always recommend having a religious symbol in your car. I recommend placing a rosary, a placard, or a small statue on your dash that will help keep them away. I recommend wearing a cross or religious symbol around your neck, so they will not bother you.

When people do not understand something, and they cannot control someone else, or they feel threatened, they try to stop people from doing certain things. The

Catholic Church is a good example of this. They look upon people with psychic and mediumship abilities, such as me, as talking with or working with the devil. They know very well that this is not the case because every Catholic priest is trained in mediumship and psychic development. They are also trained on how to recognize demonic possession and how to perform an exorcism. If they excel in that area it becomes their full-time job. In fact, there have been so many demonic possessions as of late, and so few priests doing that work, that the church cannot keep up.

A few years ago, the Catholic Church started training laymen to perform the ritual of exorcism. The reason they do not want everyone else using their psychic and mediumship abilities, however, again, has to do with control and the Catholic Church wanting to appear superior. They are not the only organized religion that takes the same position for the same reason. Many people in positions of power have difficulty handling the power and that is also true for organized religions.

Eventually, I found my life path of teaching people. I teach them to understand that their soul is pure energy, how to connect with their soul, and how energy works. I teach them how to get out of their brain, and to live a loving and fulfilling life while learning the five love lessons that they came here for. I ended up specializing in relationships and created a seven-week Relationship

Mastery Program to teach people how the Universe works, and how to change their energy.

We are all like magnets, and we are either repelling or attracting people, events, and objects into our lives at all times. You may or may not stay in the same relationship after your energy changes, and you understand your love lessons, but you will understand why you were together. You will understand what you needed to learn—or what the other person needed to learn—and be able to move on to the next chapter of your life with a whole new perspective. When you learn the five love lessons and raise your vibration, you live from a higher vantage point, you see things from a different perspective, and you can then easily manifest all the wonderful things that bring you happiness and joy into your world.

Karma And Our Lessons

Most of us have karma[2] to clear from our past lifetimes; it is one of the many reasons we come back and reincarnate. If someone wronged you in a past life and they did not make amends, they need to come back in another lifetime to correct the wrong. They have built up karma that they owe you. If we have not made amends in our own past lives, we may owe someone else whom we are making amends for in this lifetime. This is a karmic debt that you owe someone. Always try and make amends in this lifetime so you do not create more karma for yourself. If you have wronged someone in some way, make sure they know you are sorry and have regrets. If you have stolen something from someone, replace it, and make amends.

---

[2] Karma is a concept with a few definitions, specifically in Hinduism and Buddhism, and the common sayings "what goes around comes around" and "what you sow is what you reap" are great examples of how karma works.

Hinduism identifies karma as the relationship between a person's mental or physical action and the consequences following that action. It also signifies the consequences of all the actions of a person in their current and previous lives and the chain of cause and effect in morality. https://www.webmd.com/balance/what-is-karma

Many times, you will get into a relationship with someone that has a karmic connection to either fix a wrong from a past lifetime or help you in this lifetime because they owe you, or you owe them. While the karmic debt is being repaid, one or both of you are learning a lesson. Maybe the person you were in a romantic relationship with during a past lifetime cheated on you. You will come into this lifetime to cheat on the reincarnation of that person so they can experience what it felt like to have it done to them. Those relationships are strictly to teach one, or both of you, one of the lessons you need to learn and repay a past debt. That way, you experience what you caused that person, and the scales are now balanced.

Everything in the Universe needs to always stay in balance. Your karmic debt is now repaid to that person, and hopefully, you are on your way to learning one of the love lessons that you needed to learn. In a cheating situation, it could be self-worth, or it could be unconditional love. The person being cheated on also has to learn that it is never about them specifically or anything they did. It is always something that is supposed to happen according to the life paths you both chose. We are always right where we are supposed to be at any given time.

There is always the possibility, however, that you just wanted to experience what it felt like without it being connected to past karma. The problem with that is that you just created future karma unless you show remorse toward the person you just cheated on. The only way to really know for sure what the reason was is to go back and read your Akashic records, also known as your book of life. Needless to say, almost everyone's life is complicated because we chose to have it that way. If you chose a simple life, it would not be as exciting, and you probably would not learn as much or as quickly. The more advanced the soul, I find the more challenging the lifetime plan.

There are five major love lessons that people's souls will have to learn, if not in this lifetime, in the next, or the next. It is entirely up to you whether you choose to learn them now or not. Some people are very stubborn and learn slower than others. The Universe always gives us the gift of choice, however. If you choose to delay your lessons, you can; they will just spill over into your next lifetime.

A lot of people feel that if they cannot see something, or touch it, it is not real. I used to be one of those people. Let me remind those people that they cannot see or touch air, but they are all breathing it. You cannot see or touch the microwaves cooking your food, but something sure makes it hot when you push that button! Just because you cannot see or feel it in your present state does not mean energy and souls are not real.

Some people need to learn more than one love lesson, and some people seem to need to learn all five of them. We learn things much faster within a relationship, whether it is a love relationship that is romantically, or sexually involved, or a relationship with friends or family. We also learn things much faster here on Earth than on the other side. If we do not learn the lesson we will keep repeating the same type of relationship over and over again until we learn the lesson. Many times, you do not realize you are a creature of habit, and you are repeating a pattern, but those around you will see it.

Did you ever date someone who looked and acted just like an ex-husband or an ex-wife? Or maybe all your girlfriends or boyfriends seem to be the same "type." Your friends notice the resemblance or the same habits, but you just did not see it. You are following a pattern of repeating the same scenario with another person because you did not learn the lesson you were supposed to learn the first time around. The Universe actually places a veil around you so you do not see the resemblance until you are supposed to. So, it is actually okay; there are no accidents in this world and no coincidences, and you planned on being a slower learner for some reason. Maybe you wanted to savor the experiences more. Before I give you what the lessons are, let me expound a bit on the relationship types you will encounter during your lifetime.

Relationship Types

Twin Flames

There are three major types of relationships people can be involved in. A twin-flame relationship, which is extremely rare, is where one's soul literally splits into two different bodies prior to reincarnation. Your soul comes here in two different bodies to have more experiences than one's normal soul would have, as well as other various reasons, depending upon the person.

I myself am a "twin flame," not in a union, but I have met my other half. I was taken back into my Akashic records to learn that I decided to have my soul split into two after living a lifetime as a man who had no one in his life who loved him. I was an orphaned child who grew up on the streets and lived a meager life, living under the stairs at a pub. I did miscellaneous jobs for the pub owner, who in turn fed me and gave me a place to sleep and clothes to wear. I would see people who were coupled up, holding hands, and having children together. I spent my whole life alone, never experiencing a sexual relationship or even a kiss with a woman.

My soul did not want to live that existence again, not knowing what it was to experience love, so it split into two souls before reincarnating again. That way, there would always be some other person with part of my soul—my twin flame—who would be a "her" on earth and would help me in some way and truly love me. That was many reincarnations ago, and I have gone through many lifetimes, finding my twin flame in every lifetime.

These are very rare relationships; they are very advanced souls, and not everyone has a twin flame. There are many different opinions out there on the subject, and since I receive my information directly from the other side, I would say the other opinions are not accurate. In my understanding, there are only a limited number of twin flames on the earth at any given time. The lessons that these people learn here are much more difficult and much more complicated than those of the average person. They are not the romantic relationship depicted in movies like *The Notebook*. They are a blend of a karmic and a soulmate relationship on steroids! They feel things on a much deeper level than most people and have an extremely intense psychic connection with each other since they actually share a part of each other's soul.

Twin-flame relationships are not something that always ends up in union in the present lifetime because the lessons that they are learning here—basically, how to enlighten the world and change humanity—can be overwhelming. These are lessons over and above the five main love lessons that everyone has to learn. In fact, most twin flames do not reunite on earth, but on the other side, because one or both cannot learn all the love lessons they need to learn here and accomplish what they came here for. They will always find each other at a pre-determined time in life, and that meeting will change the entire trajectory of each other's lives. The meeting, although fairly brief, will initiate a spiritual awakening and completely change their life paths, putting them on the path of helping others.

Twin-flame relationships are always sexual, very intense, and very brief. They usually do not last more than a few weeks to a few months but will leave an intense impression on both parties. They are required to split up after the brief connection, however, so they can both do the work they came here for. They need to do some kind of work to help further humanity. Once they have accomplished getting on their life path, they will have another opportunity later in life to connect again. If either of the people has not learned the five lessons, they will end up blocking the reunion. They share an advanced psychic connection and will always be able to feel the other person, even if one or the other does not recognize what they are connecting to and feeling.

Soulmates

A soulmate relationship is what most people have experienced and is among the most desirable of relationships. You know someone is a soulmate because they just feel really good to be around, like wearing an old pair of shoes or slippers. It is a very comfortable relationship, and it feels like you have known the person for a much longer period of time than you actually have. You really seem to click right away and have a lot of things in common. The relationship seems to flow naturally, and fairly quickly. Your soulmate is here to help teach you lessons and also to afford you a lot of comfort and love. A soulmate can come in many different forms, such as a pet, a family member, an intimate relationship, or a good friend. They are not just lovers or in an intimate relationship. Even after learning your lesson, a soulmate relationship will continue to grow.

Not all soulmate relationships last forever, but they can. It really depends on what plan you designed for yourself. We all also have many soulmates on earth with us, not just a few. The odds are pretty good that you will have a lot of wonderful soulmate relationships during your lifetime. If it is a romantic or sexual relationship, you will both help each other to learn the love lessons that you still need to learn here. The relationship will not be wine and roses all the time, but you will have a strong knowledge that you belong together. You will still have misunderstandings and quarrels, but each time you reconnect you should be getting closer to the love lesson you are learning. Once you learn the five love lessons, life, and all relationships that you allow into your life, will become much more meaningful. Life itself will become less stressful because you can see things from a higher and different perspective.

Karmic Relationship

Last, but not least, is a karmic relationship. A karmic relationship never really feels comfortable like a soulmate relationship does. The other person always seems to be keeping you on your guard and gives you a feeling that you are being challenged in some way. It is almost like you are always looking for the other shoe to drop, or constantly looking over your shoulder. Believe it or not, you seem to learn the most difficult of your lessons within a karmic relationship. Once one or both of the people in the karmic relationship learn their lessons, the relationship ends. You may have completely different lessons to learn, but once you both learn them, you practically look at each other one morning and wonder why you are even together. Karmic relationships can last a long time if one or both of you are extremely stubborn and are resisting learning what it is you are there for. If one of the people in a karmic relationship learned their lesson and the other did not, the relationship usually ends, but not amicably. The person who has not learned their lesson will continue on to the next person and the next relationship until they learn the lesson the Universe is trying to teach them.

In all relationships, there is a leader and a follower. There is one person who is in charge of the relationship and makes most of the decisions within the relationship—that is the leader. Even if the other person feels like they are in charge of the relationship, they really are not. If the relationship ends, it is because the leader's soul has decided it is time. The follower may want it to end as well, but the decision always rests with the leader. How is it determined who is the leader and who is the follower? It is much more complicated than what I would be able to explain here. It has to do with a combination of astrology and numerology to determine which of you is the leader, and every relationship is different.

So Why Are We Here?

We are all eternal beings, a soul in a body, if you will, just like an avatar. Our soul is who we really are, not the body that we chose to be in. It's like driving a car; the car is just the vehicle to get your body around somewhere. Your body is the vehicle to carry around your soul. Your soul is also much bigger than your body. People talk about seeing an aura over someone's head; that is the part of their soul right outside of their body. The different colors of the aura are due to the person's energetic vibration. The brighter the color is, the higher the vibration. White light is the highest, next is gold, and so on down the line.

Many people will research auras and say that certain colors mean you are artistic, musical, thoughtful, etc. My experience is that it has more to do with your energetic vibration. I believe the other meanings they are applying are psychic impressions they are picking up on the person themselves. The majority of your soul is in the lowest level of heaven, also known as the fifth dimension. That part of your soul, known as your higher self, is what orchestrates the timing of all the events in your life. We are in the third dimension; your dream state is in the fourth dimension, and the fifth dimension is the lowest level of heaven.

When mediums such as myself contact souls from the other side, we raise our vibration and they lower theirs so that we can meet in the fourth dimension, the dream state. If you are not in touch with your soul, your true self, you might have a lot of interesting experiences in your dream state. That is the fourth dimension, and it will be the easiest place for your soul to connect with you. Other souls that have passed to heaven, and even souls from living people, will also come to you in your dream state to bring you messages and information that they feel you need to know. You will know it is a "visit," and not a dream because it will not only seem real, but you will wake up as soon as the visit is over, and you will remember it. Make sure to write it down because you may not remember all the details once you go back to sleep.

Some of your soul also leaves your body, if it so chooses, to go and visit others as well. If you think you are dreaming about a conversation, or seeing something or someone, it feels like it is real, and you wake up right away, it is your soul traveling. If you learn how to practice meditation on a regular basis (I will teach you later in the book), you will be able to see and converse with these souls during the day when you're awake, and they won't feel the need to contact you as often when you're trying to sleep.

The human body is a wonderful, very complicated, achievement. Your brain is an amazing computer. It has the ability to rewire itself if damaged, and it performs wonderfully complicated feats. People who have been involved in car accidents and have traumatic brain injuries can regain a good portion of their abilities in time. That is because the brain will rewire itself around the damaged areas. It is not your soul, however, or who you are; the brain is just there to process the information that you learn. It also has a primary job beyond processing information, however.

What is the primary purpose of your brain? It is to protect your body. How does the brain do that? It does it by creating fear. Most people go through their whole life making their decisions based on fear. Look at the supposed Covid pandemic we recently went through. How were they able to push the agenda so quickly? They did it by supplying misinformation and playing to people's fear of the unknown.

Knowledge is power; it keeps you from living in fear. When you learn the five love lessons, you live a life without fear because you rely on the "knowing" of your soul and the trusting that there is a higher power with your best interest at heart.

Have you ever just had a "knowing" that there was something that you needed to do? You didn't think about it a lot, you just did it, and it worked out fine. Maybe it was to take a certain job, marry a certain person, or move to a certain area. Maybe it was just to drive in a different direction than you usually go to get to work. You listened to your "knowing," and you avoided a major accident.

When you have a "knowing," that's your soul communicating with you, not your brain. When you make a decision from your soul, it will be the right decision one hundred percent of the time. It will always work out for the best, even if you cannot see it at the moment. Maybe you married someone because you knew it was the right thing to do at the time. Perhaps you got divorced at a later time, so you are thinking that it was not the right decision. But maybe you had children with that person that you could not have had with someone else. Maybe you learned one of your love lessons with this person. It is always the correct decision if it is made with your soul.

Your soul wants to protect you more than your brain but needs to always keep you on your life path and the plan you made for yourself before coming here. When you make a decision with your brain, however, it is literally a crapshoot. Sometimes it is the right decision and sometimes it is not. Usually, you question whether or not you made the right decision. When it is a "knowing," made with your soul, you do not question the decision, you just do it. Your brain will always help you work out the details when you are following your soul, and when you follow your soul, your decision will always work out for your best.

I went as far as opening a five-thousand-square-foot daycare center with next to no money and three children while going through a divorce because I "knew" it was the right thing to do. I could not find decent daycare for my ten-month-old son, and I had to go back to work because of the divorce. I just knew I was supposed to open a daycare, even though I had no experience in the field, and I only had ten thousand dollars saved from working two jobs.

Not only did I open the business and buy the building after the first year, but it is what set me on my path to making my fortune in real estate and business. I opened a second location in another state within three years and operated them both for over thirteen years. Everyone thought I was absolutely insane to take on such a large undertaking, but I just "knew" in my soul it was what I was supposed to do. I was almost like a horse with blinders on; I could only see forward, and I had a deep "knowing" that it was the right thing to do. Apparently, I was on my soul path because although it was very challenging, it worked out better than I could have ever imagined. All the pieces just continued to fall into place. That is a great indicator that you are on the right soul path.

The way you connect to your soul on a regular basis is through meditation. You have to get out of your "computer" head. You need to let go of "your" thoughts in order for the soul's messages to come through. Most people pray or ask the Universe or a higher power to help with something. When you pray, you are asking. When you meditate, you are listening and getting your answers.

It is very important to protect yourself prior to meditation, however. There is a lot of evil in this world, and when you open yourself up to the Universe through meditation, you are opening yourself up, not just to good, but to evil as well. The whole game of good and evil is about how many souls they can collect. If you have a pure heart and are connecting to your soul, you become a target for evil. In later chapters, I will teach you how to meditate properly, how to understand, and how to listen to what the Universe is trying to tell you.

How Does Energy Affect Us?

Everything in the Universe is made of pure energy. There are lower vibrations and higher vibrations. Lower vibrations repel things from coming into our life, and higher vibrations attract like magnets. Many people have heard of the "law of attraction." This is the concept. However, in order for it to work and be lasting you need to permanently change your energy. Changing your energy is not an easy process; hence, the reason I developed a seven-week program to teach people how to do that.

Learning your five love lessons is a big part of changing your energy and raising your vibration. We are all made of energy, and our souls are pure energy. If you have ever thought about someone, and then they either called or showed up, it is because *thoughts are things*, and where your thoughts go your energy flows.

I have helped thousands of people raise their vibrations and get in touch with their souls to understand their path in life, what love lessons they came here to learn, and why they are here. I have helped them to see their life from a higher perspective, to understand why things are happening in their life, and to learn that the only control they have is over their own decisions and reactions.

We have no control over anyone else's decisions or reactions. We are not responsible for how other people feel or for the decisions they make in their life. If we were able to make someone feel happy or sad, we would be able to make the person we want to love us, love us. We cannot make someone feel anything; it is on each person to be responsible for how they feel. Feelings are their reaction to their emotion.

People change all the time. They are not necessarily who you thought them to be, and sayings like "once a cheater, always a cheater" are not always true. You are not the same person you were yesterday, or even before picking up this book. When your energy changes, you will attract more people into your life on the same energetic frequency. It is like a radio station; you cannot get the station in if it is not on the right frequency. People's energy works the same way. When you change the way you do things, and the way you see things, the people around you will begin to change as well.

For every action, there is an equal or greater reaction. That is why it only takes one person to make or break a relationship and cause change in any situation. We are all like pebbles thrown into a pond. Everything you do creates a ripple effect that continues to affect the next person and the next person. At the end of the day, however, what is meant to be, will be. The choice that we have in life is whether or not we choose to learn our love lessons or we choose to delay them. You can delay them and keep repeating the same things over and over, even into the next lifetime, or you can learn your love lessons, understand your purpose here, and live an absolutely amazing life! Now, let us talk about the lessons you came here for.

Our Love Lessons Detailed

Love Lesson 1: Self-worth

One of the most common lessons in life that we need to learn is to understand our own self-worth. Most people need to learn how to put themselves first. It is not selfish or narcissistic to put yourself first; this is where everything else comes from. If you are on an airplane and the airbag comes down, you need to put it on yourself before putting it on another person. You cannot help someone else if you cannot breathe. If you cannot be good to yourself, and take care of yourself, you will not have the energy, money, or health to take care of another person. It is not a justification to treat other people poorly or to become selfish. It is, however, knowing that you are not going to sacrifice your desires and happiness to placate another person.

You were not put here to be a martyr or to sacrifice your happiness. All relationships are built on compromise, but when you are compromising too much, that is an indicator that you are not in the right relationship. Not all relationships—whether romantic or friendships— are made to last forever. Maybe the lesson has been learned and the relationship has run its course. If you are not happy, and the relationship does not bring joy into your life, it is time to move on.

Of all the love lessons for people to learn, self-worth seems to be one of the most challenging. Every person on the face of the earth deserves to be loved, cherished, and happy. It is not something that you have to earn, and it is not something that you can buy, it is your birthright. You are unique, and since you are unique, you have value like no other person. There is only one of you in the whole world. People who do not value themselves or love themselves keep seeking approval from other people. This is a result of many different things, but most likely part of their upbringing and life plan.

If when you were young and growing up, you did not feel that you were loved and cherished, the result of that is feeling that you have no value and no self-worth. You feel that you do not deserve love and happiness. As much as outside forces influence how we feel, the reality is that knowing what you deserve, valuing yourself, and being happy is an inside job. No one else is responsible for your happiness but you and no one can make you happy but you. When two people are each happy individually, they can attract each other with their energy, like magnets, and the happiness and love will ping pong back and forth between them. Just as you do not have the power to make someone love you or want to be with you, they do not have the power to make you happy or sad. Those are your feelings and your responsibility. Not that they are not valid feelings, but you do not have carte blanche to wallow in the emotions forever. Give yourself a short ten-minute pity party to express them, then pick yourself up and move on with what you really deserve. Otherwise, you'll end up lowering your vibration.

When you learn to value yourself, you raise your vibration and become a very happy, joyful person. You can then attract what you want and deserve into your life—someone on the same energetic frequency as you.

It's like a radio station; you cannot get the station in if you are not on the right frequency. Life and love work the same way. You attract everything into your life that is on the same frequency as you. You have to be able to love yourself before you're able to love someone else. Otherwise, subconsciously, you continue to look for someone who can teach you how to value and love yourself.

If you are not learning the love lesson, you will continue to play the *poor me* card, claiming that things are happening to you because you are no good, or you do not deserve good things in your life. This is a lower vibrational attitude that will end up repelling higher vibrational people from you, not attracting them like a magnet.

Where does all this lack of self-worth come from? It mostly comes from growing up in the family that you chose to be with. (We plan this life before we come here and plan the lessons we will learn as well as the people we will interact with.) There are many different ways that this manifests in a relationship. Let us start first with your possible family dynamic.

If you grew up in a family where, as a child, you felt your parents did not care, you were not heard, and you were not listened to, most likely, you felt that you had no value. It is more than likely your parents did not love themselves and maybe not even each other. Children do learn what they live and imitate what they see. Most likely, your parents grew up in a generation that was not very touchy-feely. They probably did not get hugs from their parents and were never told they were loved.

Older generations assumed that if there was a roof over your head and food on the table, it was proof of love and value. Unfortunately, as children growing up, we need constant reinforcement that when we make mistakes or do something our parents do not approve of, we are still loved and have value. If you don't receive the examples somewhere else and are able to see beyond your parent's actions, you'll continue the pattern of not loving yourself and feeling unvalued. You will then continue the cycle with your own children unless you recognize the pattern and make an effort to change it. Any pattern can be broken if it is recognized and you have the desire and willpower to make the change.

My parents were both of German decent and both grew up in very cold, unexpressive families. Their parents never hugged them or told them that they loved them. My mother found out late in life that she had been adopted. As a child, she always felt that something was wrong with her because her mother treated her very differently than she did her siblings. She was always left out of events and never told that she was loved or hugged. Her brother and sister, however, got hugged in front of her often. This left my mother with the deep impression of not being valued or loved. From a very young age, she felt like she did not belong.

My father's father—my grandfather—died when my father was very young. This left him without a male role model and a mother who was cold and indifferent toward him. He joined the Navy at a young age and lived his life believing that females were only good for sex and having babies. Apparently, he was abused somewhere along the line because he had a very controlling attitude with his family, abusive and not loving.

Being one of eight children, and having parents that were not only not loving, but also abusive, it was many years before I found my self-worth. My father would tell the girls that their only value was to have sex and babies. He would say that only the boys had value because they carried on the family name. He was definitely a misogynist. Only after I became a successful businesswoman and bailed my father out financially, did he begin to see my value. It was always a backhanded compliment that he gave me, however. He would tell me how proud he was of me but then he would say that I should have been born a boy.

Fortunately, I had found my self-worth by that time and was able to counter his words by telling him how proud I was of myself as a successful woman, that I was proud to have achieved what I did with no help from him, and I was proud of myself no matter what he thought. My parents never told me they loved me, nor hugged me until I was around thirty years old. I gave them each a hug at different times and told them I loved them. Each of them thanked me and cried. Every time I saw them, I hugged them before leaving and let them know that I loved them. It wasn't something they were used to, but they both needed to feel the human connection.

Suppose you are an only child. Most likely, when you were younger, your parents probably doted on you because you were the only one they had. They made you feel special, giving you attention and gifts. As you got older, however, they got tired of that. Maybe they found other interests, but you missed getting all of that attention. Somewhere inside, you felt that you were not measuring up since they did not pay as much attention to you anymore. Or they put so much pressure on you, since you were their only focus of attention, that it was impossible to meet their high standards. Maybe they expected you to be a high achiever. You started to believe that you were unworthy of love because no matter how much you did, it seemed like you were criticized and told to do better. No matter how hard you tried, they seemed to always expect more. They may have also kept treating you like an annoyance because, to them, you were an intrusion on their time.

You may not even have had the opportunity to be a child. Many children with no siblings are treated like mini-adults. Their parents don't play with them, and they often include them with all their adult friends and activities.

Perhaps you grew up in a large family. With so many children vying for your parent's attention, you may have felt that you were lost in the bustle of things. The atmosphere itself could have been very chaotic. You may have felt that your siblings were getting more attention and were loved more than you were by your parents. You may also have been bullied, abused, or neglected by your siblings, and possibly your parents as well.

All of these things can lead you to feel that you are not worthy of love. They will also create a dysfunctional atmosphere that you may become comfortable with. When this happens, you continue to be drawn to chaos so that you don't have to focus on yourself and learn the love lesson. It becomes your unhealthy comfort zone. In that zone, you will find that you attract dysfunctional relationships because they feel familiar.

A lot of children are physically, verbally, or sexually abused. When you are young and forming connections with people, and you are being hurt continuously by people who are supposed to love you and care for you, you decide that this is happening because you have no worth. They may tell you straight out that they do not love you and that they never wanted you. The more extreme the abuse, the more challenging it is to overcome.

Remember, you chose the life and the lessons; you also chose the difficulty level you wanted to handle. This means that there is nothing that you cannot overcome. Believe it or not, you wanted the challenge.

You also need to remember that what other people think about you, or say about you, is not your business. Everyone is entitled to their own opinion, just as you are. You do not need to change their minds. Those people do not matter. What matters is that you know who you are and that you love yourself. The right people who are supposed to be in your life will find a way to be there.

People will do different things when they feel that they are not valued and they have no self-worth. They may act out within the family and take it out on the people they really love the most. They may yell at or physically abuse their children or their spouse. Many people feel a lot of anger toward the people who did not give them the love they needed and wanted. Some people alienate their family members because the memory of the pain is just too great, or they blame others for their unhappiness. Other people will have lifelong jealousy issues with their siblings. Some people turn to drugs and alcohol to dull the pain they feel.

All the relationships you get into from this point forward will be trying to teach you that you have value and deserve to be loved. The happiness you seek, however, will not come until you love and value yourself. Until that point, there may be a lot of codependent relationships. These relationships will enable you to not learn your lesson, and you will stop the other person from learning theirs. Once you learn your lesson, this will all change and fall away. You will be able to let go with love and understanding.

Everyone handles learning the lesson in a different manner. Some people may try to get on sports teams to prove that they have ability and value. They may be very good athletically, and by achieving, they get the recognition that makes them feel better. If they fail, however, or get older and have to stop the activity, and have not learned the lesson of loving themselves, it will be that much harder to overcome all of that inner negativity.

Other people become overachievers at school or work, trying to get praise from higher-ups and family. They still do not love themselves; they are looking for love from outside of themselves. A lot of people follow career paths that they do not like and do not want to be in to make their parents or someone else happy. Then they feel that no matter what they do, they are not ever good enough, since it was not done for their own happiness. They did it to get their parents or someone else's love and attention.

Many people will go straight from an unhappy childhood to looking for a partner in life, trying to find love. They look for someone who can fill in the voids and love them the way they do not love themselves. It may not work out, because it is not a healthy relationship, but they are following a repeating pattern. They did not learn to love themselves from their parents, hence, the reason that many children marry someone who acts very similar to their own parents. There is some truth to the saying that a girl will always marry her father and a boy his mother. Although you do not, other people may recognize that the person in your life has the same behaviors as a parent or resembles them in some way. If their father was a verbally abusive or violent person, many people will accept that behavior in their relationship with a significant other. Either they will be the abusive party, or the mate they choose will be abusive in some manner. If the mother was the abusive person, the daughter is more likely to emulate those behaviors, or if the son was trying to gain her acceptance, he will follow the abusive pattern. They will either take it out on their mate or their children.

Children do learn what they live and they will repeat the cycle. If you grew up in chaos, you may choose a situation that is chaotic. Maybe you will choose to date someone who has a sketchy living situation, multiple children, or some mental illness. If you love yourself and know your self-worth, you will not get into those situations any longer. You will not attract chaos with a higher vibration, and you will understand that you deserve better.

Self-worth and self-esteem are very much tied together. Self-esteem is what we feel and believe about ourselves, and how we think others see us. Self-worth is the "knowing" that we are bigger than even what we think and that we have an incomprehensible value. Our Creator does not make mistakes.

No one said the work would be easy, but it is well worth the reward. Many people will have multiple relationships and marriages with people who either resemble the previous person or physically act like the previous person. This is because the dysfunction you grew up with has become your comfort zone. You have to recognize that the pattern you are following is not a healthy one, and it is not conducive to living the loving, happy life that you deserve. If it does not "feel" good, then it is not good. Part of learning the five love lessons is being able to listen to your soul and recognize when it is time to move on and time to let go.

Many people will stay in a dysfunctional relationship, playing the martyr, and using excuses like they are staying for the children, or that it is too expensive to get a divorce or to separate. These people are doing a disservice to everyone else in the family since the children will learn to repeat the cycle, and they are also delaying their lessons.

Unless the Universe steps in to make the change for you without your consent or input, you can delay your lessons from lifetime to lifetime if you are too lazy or too stubborn. Some people actually write the script for the Universe to step in if they cannot do it themselves. Then something major will happen to facilitate the next step. Maybe the other person learns their lesson first and leaves or a job takes you away from the situation and introduces you to another person who can help you. Maybe the other person dies and goes on to their rewards in heaven. You always have to stay open to what the Universe does for you since it is always working for your highest and best outcome in any given situation.

When you learn your value, love yourself, and become happy with yourself and your life, you raise the vibration of your energy. Remember that we are like magnets. We are always either attracting or repelling at any given time. When you are attracting with a high vibration, the Universe reaches down to help you achieve anything you want in this world. You just need to reach back. Everything you desire will then start entering your life. It is like Christmas every day. Whether it is a new job, a new house, a new car, or just wanting to have peace in your life, anything, and everything you want is there for the asking.

Just remember to be grateful as you start to receive what it is you have been asking for. As much as you may feel you have done it on your own, you really have not. There are many souls, angels, and higher powers helping you on this side and from the other side.

Love Lesson 2: Money and Balance

Many people have to learn the lessons of money and balance. Too many people put a higher value on money than on their families, loved ones, friends, and their own health. Remember that money is energy; that is why it is called currency. Many times, this lesson is tied to your self-worth and will either lead you to that lesson or reinforce what you have already learned. Money is a means to an end and helps things stay in balance.

The Universe itself needs to always stay in balance. This is why you see the scales of justice, or the yin-yang. Every culture speaks of it and practices it in many forms. For everything you give, you will receive. Hence, the reason when you buy items like groceries, or have a service from someone, you pay with money. There has always been some kind of barter system in place, even before civilizations created paper money. The Indians used to trade jewelry until they developed wampum. Older civilizations used gold and silver.

You may also use a barter system in place of money to keep things balanced. Many ancient civilizations started with that before developing a monetary system and would trade furs and food. Many professionals nowadays will trade services with each other. They make sure that the services they barter are of equal value to both parties. There are barter sites on the internet that people go to, just as there are selling sites. Instead of money, you barter items of equal value. When people value money too much, it can become out of balance. It does not determine your value, only your net worth on a balance sheet. It is not something you can take with you when you go to the other side, and it is not meant to be hoarded. Not to say you cannot save it, but the more you put out into the Universe, that much more will come back to you. It is actually how all energy works: the love you put out is equal to the love you will receive.

We are all meant to share what we have an abundance of, whether it is knowledge, money, or energy of another form like food. A calorie is a measurement of the energy, or fuel, in food. No one person is an island, and we all affect many other people, even if we do not realize it. You may be the kind word that stops someone from jumping off of a bridge or the person that gives hope to someone who has been struggling for a long time.

We are here to always help others in any way possible. It costs nothing to be kind and will continually raise, not only your vibration but the energetic vibration of everyone around you. What you put out, you get back in a larger way. I have had my life changed in a massive direction because I knew someone who was the kindest, most giving person I had ever met. They had no idea the impression they left upon me, that not even having them in my life still led me to be a better person and achieve a greater level of awareness. Every life affects many other lives.

The Universe makes sure that you always have money for the necessities of life, provided you do your part. You cannot sit on your couch all day and ask the Universe to bring you a job without opening the newspaper or looking on the help-wanted site on the internet. The Universe will always make sure you are provided for, but you need to do your part as well. Money also needs to be respected. You should always be aware of the money you have in your wallet or purse. It should be neatly arranged and not just crumbled up and thrown in a pocket or a purse. Like everything the Universe gives us, money needs to be taken care of, and you need to show that you are grateful for it. If you do not appreciate what you have, the Universe takes notice and will make sure you get less, not more, so "pay" attention. No pun intended.

Let's say you grew up very poor; you may become a miser of money, so you just save your money and never spend it. Not only are you not valuing yourself enough to enjoy the fruits of your labor, but this will also start to alienate the people around you. The reason for that, again, is from being out of balance. Instead of having positive energy around you, you will have a buildup of negative energy. Instead of attracting, you will start to repel; your magnet will be flipped. Most people who are hoarding their money are not happy and do not trust the people around them.

Many are afraid they are liked because of their money, or that the people around them want to steal their money. This, again, ties into self-worth and trust. They believe that their friends and family would not want them or love them if they had no money. They also do not trust the Universe to make sure that they will have what they need. Clearly, they are having difficulty learning the five love lessons they came here for.

Many people feel guilty, maybe because they had other priorities than their family or loved ones when they were starting off in their careers. Maybe they were obsessed with earning as much money as possible at the expense of their own well-being and that of their friends and family. Maybe they spent all their time working, so their downtime was spent getting enough sleep to just go back to work again. They didn't spend any time with their partner or children. A lot of people who have done this now try to assuage their guilt with money. They start giving money or gifts to the people they neglected—their spouse, their children, their parents—to make up for the time they did not spend with them.

Money cannot replace your time with someone; they want to be with you, not your money. Money cannot keep you warm at night or keep you company.

Perhaps you are an absent parent, and you do not really spend any time with your children. Or maybe you are a non-custodial parent and you do not take your children when you are supposed to. You may think that giving them money or buying them things will make up for your lack of time.

Money cannot buy love or happiness, and by substituting money for love, you are creating an imbalance. The children are not actually giving you anything in return. It leads to more self-worth issues on their part and starts a repeat of a cycle. It also teaches them that money does not have to be earned and creates a further imbalance in their lives.

Money is not meant to be a replacement, and if not used properly, it takes things to a whole new level of dysfunction. It cannot replace the things that are missing in our lives, like communication, spending time together, health, love, and affection. You can have all the money in the world and still be lonely and unhappy.

Many people will work too much, just to save more money than they need. They feel a lack of something in their life, and they think by over-saving, they can fill the void. They may be equating their self-worth with money as well. They may also be living in fear of having a lack of money someday. This also creates an imbalance of time that you do not have to spend with family and loved ones or to take care of yourself and do the things that you enjoy.

Money cannot buy happiness, health, or more time. There are many people who live a minimalist lifestyle and are extremely happy people. If you are already happy with yourself, then money is just more energy to use and do things to share your happiness with others. If you are unhappy and have money, you may find yourself spending it frivolously, trying to buy happiness. You may get involved with prostitutes, drugs, or alcohol, thinking that it is the answer or the road to happiness. You have to find the balance in your life so that you are not living to work but working to live and realize money is not just a means to an end but to be enjoyed while on your journey of life.

Some of this might, again, be a pattern that was learned in childhood. Years ago, when we were young, there was usually only one person working in the family, so they had to work more to afford a better lifestyle. Through the generations, however, prices increased, and both parents in the family had to work to afford a family. Then it went from just buying a house and car to having the newest play station and a flat-screen television set for each person in the family. Less time was spent with spouses and children, and the family unit started to deteriorate. Money became the priority.

Some countries other than the United States do not seem to have the same value system when it comes to money. In those countries, most people are content to have just what they need, with the possibility of a little extra. They do not have a lot of opportunities to bring in larger sums of money, so they make sure that they spend time with their family when they are not working. Many do not own cars because of the costs involved, and they manage within their means. They also do not spend their money on "stuff" just for the sake of buying. Not only can they not afford it, but they also may have no place to put it. They use any spare money they have to go out to dinner or do something as a family so that they can enjoy the experience together.

The United States seems to have possibly become the most materialistic of societies. Many people in the U.S. feel that they never have enough money and always want more, even to the point of families trying to "keep up with the Jones" so the family does not feel somehow deprived. They have to have bigger and better than the next family so they will "fit in," so others do not see them as having less value. Every generation wants their children to have more and struggle less. The problem with that, however, is that the children do not value what they have when they did not have to earn it. This is not in balance; it now repeats the cycle and leads the children to their unrealistic lessons surrounding money and balance because it was not taught at home.

Money does not change the way you live your life, it just allows you to live it in a larger lifestyle. However, many people see money to be used as a tool to achieve power. If money is not used properly, it will lower your vibration and create an abusive situation. Many people do not know how to handle large sums of money. Statistically, most multi-million-dollar-plus lottery winners are flat-broke or dead within five years of winning. They start spending time with people who will help them spend it on things to self-abuse, like drugs, alcohol, or prostitutes.

Other people with a monetary imbalance may start abusing the other person in their relationship by not sharing any of the money that they have because it jeopardizes them in the powerful position of being the provider. Many men and women live in fear of someone coming into their life to take all of their money, and not wanting them for who they are, just for what they have. Thus, they may not be honest as to their ability to build a life that is in balance with a partner. They will not contribute in equal measure to a lifestyle that they are building together. This will eventually breed resentment and a lack of trust between both people. This, again, is not only a money issue but a self-worth and trust issue.

The same is true of someone coming into a relationship wanting to be "taken care of" financially. Unless there is a barter system in place, where that party is doing something to balance the equation, like cooking or cleaning, there will be problems because the relationship is out of balance.

Everything in the Universe needs to stay in balance. The challenge in all relationships is how to maintain that, especially when not all people earn the same amount of money. If one person is seen as contributing more time and less money, or visa-versa, it could become a problem. Money can also create a lot of fear, fear of losing all of their money or fear of someone stealing all their money.

Fear of not having enough money may make you do things you normally would not do. These are all low-vibrational perspectives that will alienate the people you care about. This all leads to either learning the lesson or reinforcing the lessons of trust.

If money is one of the lessons you need to learn, you may see that it comes and goes in large chunks in your life. Maybe you are always down to your last dollar before you sell a piece of real estate and reap the windfall rewards. Maybe you cannot seem to get ahead, and then you receive a large sum from an inheritance or lawsuit. Maybe you are constantly changing jobs, believing that the next one is more lucrative. Money is like a river, it ebbs and flows. When you realize that it is really energy (that is why it is called currency) and that you cannot take it with you, you can begin to see it from the proper perspective. The Universe will always provide for you. The more you share with others, and the more grateful you are, the more it comes back to you. What you put out to the Universe and the angels, the Universe hears. Always remember to be grateful for what you have.

Balance is the key, and that also leads to learning the lesson of communication. You can start to see how all the love lessons we have to learn are interconnected and intertwined with each other. Each lesson either brings you into the next lesson or reinforces what you have already learned. Everyone must learn all five love lessons in order to be successful.

Some people are meant to work hard for their money, and it never comes easy. They planned it that way before they came, and it is how they chose to learn their lesson about money. Other people seem to be showered with it and seem to have the golden touch. Everything they do seems to bring them a windfall. Some people were either born into a wealthy family, received an inheritance, or won a large sum in the lottery. Most of these people have an attitude of easy come and easy go since it was not something they had to go to any great lengths to acquire.

The person struggling to earn the money needs to learn trust. Trust that the Universe will always provide for what they want and need. The person who easily acquires money needs to learn the value of it and learn that it does not buy happiness. Most people who have a lot of money—unless they are sharing it with people who truly need it, or doing good deeds with it, like a philanthropist—are unhappy people. You can equate it on a smaller scale to dining alone. Doesn't it make for a much happier occasion when you share a meal with someone else? Whatever your situation, remember, money is energy. When you share it, and put it out into the world, it raises your energetic vibration and comes back to you on a larger scale.

The more you look around, the more you will see that everything everywhere needs to stay in balance. You would not know darkness if you had never seen light. You would not know sadness if you had never known happiness.

Everything has an opposite, which maintains the balance. The Japanese refer to it as the Ying and the Yang. For every high in life, there is a low. If you have ever paid attention to your own life, for every episode of something exciting in your life, there is another event that brings your emotions lower, to stay in balance. If you can keep your emotions in check you will find that the excitement might not be as much of a high, but the coming down will not be as bad either. It is about balancing your own emotions. Emotions are the physical expression of your feelings. They always need to be expressed in a healthy manner to protect the physical body.

Your own body itself needs to stay in balance. You need to have the proper ph. so you do not get yeast infections, cancer, viruses, etc. If you are walking out of balance, you will have back issues and knee problems. Every time you look at yourself in a mirror, the left-hand side of your body balances out the right-hand side.

One of the best ways to tell if you are in emotional balance is to see if the full moon affects you in any way. Do you have trouble sleeping? Are you more emotional? Do you get dizzy or disoriented? If you are anxious or depressed, you are out of balance emotionally. If you can answer yes to any of these questions, you are still not fully emotionally balanced. You may feel the pull, then meditate to get yourself back into balance. When you are balanced, you have an understanding, and your emotions and feelings are also balanced.

People who exhibit manic depression or bipolar disorder are an extreme example of a body's energy being out of balance. Whenever you overdo on any level, there is a self-correction that occurs, either on a physical or a spiritual level. If you overeat, you become overweight and have health issues. If you have an anorexic eating disorder, you become thin and deprive your body of needed nutrition, creating different but similar health issues. If you deprive yourself of sleep, you do not function well when you are awake. If you go out and party all night long, the next day your body needs to recuperate to get back into balance.

In a relationship, because you are with another person that brings more things to your attention, your imbalances will become more obvious. If they are not corrected, there will be negative results of one kind or another. Let us say you work long hours and do not spend time with your partner or family. Eventually, they will become distant and possibly leave. If you spend too much money, you will be in continuous debt and may lose everything you own.

Your imbalance in your life could be pointing you to another lesson that you need to learn. If you overeat out of loneliness or unhappiness, it could be that you do not value yourself, or have no self-worth. Spending could be connected to learning lessons about money. It could be the same if you work too much. You may feel that the only reasons people value you are based on your work performance or the amount of money you have saved.

There are many reasons that people do not have balance in their life, but the goal is to achieve it. It can be difficult to identify what exactly is out of balance in your life. This is where you have to go inside and get in touch with your soul. Find the things that are missing for you. It is not always an easy thing to identify and then bring back into balance. In fact, maintaining balance is one of the most difficult things to do once your energy actually shifts into a higher vibration. If you have identified the areas of imbalance, however, that is a huge start to getting your life and your energy back into balance.

When your life is in balance, it flows, and you do not struggle. You will always have the small ups and downs in life because the Universe will maintain that part for you. Life is a lot like a roller coaster ride. You go up, then go back down again. When you are in balance, however, you do not really notice the ups and downs, you just see them as new experiences.

The Universe will always bring you experiences; you have to reach up and allow them into your life. You also have to recognize when you begin to lose balance and make corrections. "No" is a word that should be in everyone's vocabulary and needs to be used when maintaining balance. You should not feel guilty when you are saying no to maintain your balance and put yourself first. That is your lesson, to maintain your balance, and happiness and peace within will always follow. It is not your job to make everyone happy in this world; that is not even possible. It is, however, your job to make *you* happy and balanced. No one else is responsible for making you happy but you.

Many people are empaths, and they absorb the energy from the people around them. This creates an imbalance since most of that energy is usually negative. This is why you can go out into a large crowd of people when you are out doing things like shopping and come home feeling drained and exhausted. If you do remember your science lessons from school, negative energy is actually made out of positive ions. The fastest and easiest way to neutralize that negative energy is to take a sea salt bath or rub the salt over your body prior to showering. Salt has negative ion properties that balance the energy out. Many people are drawn unconsciously to live near the coasts and the ocean since the sea air itself will have the same balancing effect.

Love Lesson 3: Trust and Communication

Every newborn child is born knowing how to trust. They trust that all of their needs will be taken care of for them. They trust their mother to feed them, cuddle them, clean them, and trust that both of their parents will show them love, affection, and protection. The same is true of fear. As a newborn child, they have none. Fear is a learned behavior. Fear is one of your brain's main functions. Other than processing information, its job is to create fear to protect you physically and mentally.

As the child grows, different experiences will have them questioning their trust and developing a sense of fear. It could be that they do not get fed when hungry or cuddled when they get hurt. It could be that no one was around to protect them from something scary when they needed it.

Whatever the experience is, we all end up developing and understanding what fear is and what a lack of trust entails. As a child learns to speak, the child begins to develop a communication style. If encouraged, they can be quite verbal and good at communicating their wants and needs with words, not just emotions. If they are stifled, however, there can become a lifelong journey of learning how to express themselves in a healthy manner and not just acting out emotionally as adults.

Many parents do not encourage the growth of their children. Just because most people can have children, does not mean that they should do so. In my experience, many people pay better attention to their pets than they do to their children. It is the rare child that claims a perfect upbringing.

As we become adults, we have to unlearn what we learned from certain situations we were brought up in.

No matter what your situation was while growing up, most people seem to come away with some form of dysfunction. If it was not learned at home, it could have been at school. Unlearning can be harder than learning for some; people as a whole do not like change.

The Universe itself will always supply you with what you need, provided you trust that it will do so. Even the beggar on the street will get a coin, a warm bed, or a meal if he trusts that it will happen. The Universe will make it available, you just need to do your part and partake. Fear is the opposite of trust. The Universe will always mirror back to you what you put out. If you put out fear, afraid of everything and everyone, you will attract people and situations that will build upon your fear and take advantage of your trust. If you learn to get in touch with your soul and learn how to listen to it, you will trust yourself enough to know who to avoid, who cannot be trusted, and to recognize dangerous situations.

One of the most common occurrences within a relationship is someone breaking the trust they have in another person. This usually begins from a lack of communication. Communication comes in many forms, including sex. Sex is just another form of communication, and if you cannot communicate outside of the bedroom, you will not be able to communicate in the bedroom. Communication can come in many forms, from regular phone calls, text messages during the day, or sending a card or flowers. Many times, it is the little things—like knowing the person is working late and offering to make dinner—that communicate the feeling that you care and that they are important to you.

With a lack of communication, however, one thing usually leads to another, and you have a chasm that develops. People need to know how you feel about them as well as your position on other issues. Do not assume they just know because you know. It should not be a guessing game, and it does not work by osmosis.

Human beings need constant reassurances, some more than others. They need to be told on a regular basis that they are important to you. This means you need to communicate verbally and with other signs and signals to the other person or people. Many times, after being with someone for a long period of time, we become complacent. We stop talking about our feelings, our wants, and our desires. We assume that the other person already knows and there is no need to verbalize them. People are always changing and growing, and if you do not grow together, you will grow apart. One day you will wake up and realize you have nothing in common anymore, and that you have been heading in two different directions.

Maybe the person that you are with has done something to break your trust, like spending all of the money or cheating on you physically or mentally with another person. The person that is spending all the money or cheating, and not being trustworthy, usually has issues with self-worth.

The problem is not "caused" by the other person. We are all responsible for our own decisions and choices. We all have our own life paths and lessons. You may be an integral part of the scenario that played out, but you are never the cause. It does not necessarily need to be the end of the relationship because you feel the other person cannot be trusted. If the love lesson is learned by the party that stepped out or created the trust issue, and the other person can see the situation from a higher perspective, the trust can be rebuilt, and it can be a better relationship than it was before. This will require a lot of communication and time to rebuild the trust. More honest communication would need to happen from both parties, a willingness to understand what was missing in the relationship, and what the love lesson was for each person.

This is where the lessons of unconditional love start to come in. You can love the person and not like what they did. If they choose to change, the trust can be rebuilt. Otherwise, you can choose to love the person you knew and the memories you shared. You can walk away with love, understanding that you were not the cause of anything. They were doing what they were supposed to be doing to learn their lessons, and it was a temporary situation. Possibly, only a karmic relationship.

Another way that trust and fear lessons arise in a relationship is through control issues. When someone does not trust, they try to stop the other person from living their life, growing as a person, and try to limit their freedom. They may be afraid you will cheat or leave them if you go out with your friends, or even get a job, in some cases. They project their fears upon you. They may even cheat or steal and accuse you of it. Many of these are the traits of a narcissist.

Narcissism is actually a mental disorder. Some people like to assume that a lot of the people they dated were narcissists, but many people are either undiagnosed or carry a lot of the same traits. Sometimes acting out violently to control the situation will also occur. This is one of the reasons there are so many cases of domestic abuse. Many people lash out at the people in their life, acting out of fear and lack of trust. This may be mistrust of themselves, lack of self-worth, or both.

You should not allow someone else to control you so that they can learn their lessons, although this is how it plays out many times. These are co-dependent relationships that people get into as a way of avoiding their lessons. If you allow it, it could be that you have a self-worth lesson to learn. When you learn how to put yourself first, and love and value yourself, you will not put yourself into these types of situations. You will be able to see the red flags and walk away, knowing you deserve better. Your soul will warn you in advance, and with a higher vibration, you will repel these types of situations instead of attracting them.

The same is true when it comes to a lack of communication in a relationship. Many times, this is either a control issue or a lack of trust. Without communication, the relationship will eventually wither and die. Communication is really the glue that holds a good relationship together. You need to be able to trust the other person in order to let them into the deep corners of your soul. To really feel the connection with the other person, you need to be able to both listen to the other person and voice your own concerns and ideas without fear. When you can communicate your fears, wants, and desires to another person, many times they can mirror back to you what makes you feel good about yourself. This is how closeness and a bond can begin to develop and lead to unconditional love. This is true in all relationships, not just sexual ones.

People all need certain things within an intimate relationship to feel fulfilled, and in order for it to whether the test of time, communication is a big one. Everything comes from communication, including sex.

Sex is just another form of communication taken to the next level. If you do not have trust within the relationship, neither person will be able to give themselves fully to the other person. Most men process things a little differently in their brains than women. Women need more verbal communication to feel fulfilled and more connected to a partner. Men are much more visual people. This is why they get more aroused when they see something sexual, but women need to hear the words. Men also feel more connected once they have the actual act of sex, and they are able to communicate better during and afterward, but a woman needs communication to get to that point.

Many people will use sex in a relationship to try to control the other person. Unless it is done in a role-play situation, it is related to fear and lack of trust. In order to have a fulfilling sex life with a partner, you need to have complete trust that it is not going to somehow be used against you at a later time. Many people withhold sex in a relationship as a form of punishing the other person. Sex between two people who care for and love each other should never be weaponized. It is the ultimate glue that holds you together through tough times. Men especially need to have sex in order to feel closely connected and to open up verbally with their partners.

If you are withholding sex, it is usually being done out of either fear that the other person does not love you, lack of trust in the person or the relationship, or control, which feeds into both. Some people who have been sexually abused have a difficult time learning trust and communication, and obviously, it inhibits the sex. As they learn their lessons and understand the why behind the abuse, they can relearn trust and communication and have a very fulfilling life for themselves and their partner.

Inevitably, the lesson is to trust that everything that is happening in your life is happening for a reason, and no matter how difficult a situation seems from the outset, it will always resolve for your highest and best outcome. Many times, you do not get to see the full results of a situation for years down the road. You planned this life, trust that your soul knows what is going on with the situation, and it will work out better than you could have ever imagined—and it will. Live without fear, knowing that a higher power is always protecting and providing for you. Listen to your soul and your gut to guide you.

Love Lesson 4: Unconditional Love/Gratitude

The highest vibration of all is unconditional love and gratitude, and it just may be the hardest of all the love lessons to learn. You literally have to get your energetic vibration up high enough to experience it. Many people do not learn this lesson until someone they truly loved passes away, like a parent, child, or spouse. Then in hindsight, they understand things, like although their parents may have made mistakes raising them and were very different people than they are, they still loved them. Many times, however, the Universe wants to make sure you are practicing it with someone who is currently in your life. This makes the lesson tougher to learn but longer lasting.

Maybe you will end up having some sort of a medical issue, and the person that is in your life ends up being the one that takes care of you physically. Or maybe your partner is the one that gets sick and even passes away. The Universe really spares no expense when it comes to teaching the love lessons. We always have to keep remembering that we were the one who wrote the script of our life.

If we really want to face it, we all have to admit that we have been slaves to our emotions at one time or another. What are emotions? Expressions of the way we feel. If someone hurts us or does something we do not like, many people immediately feel anger or hurt and they want to have revenge or inflict some kind of pain on the person that caused the problem. That is an emotional reaction, not something that comes from your soul. If you notice, given time, those emotions will subside. Your soul, on a deeper level, knows that the person is only doing what they are supposed to be doing to fulfill their obligations here and learn their lessons. It is really not about you, as much as you feel that you may be the collateral damage.

Unconditional love literally means loving without conditions. When you can look at the scenario from a higher perspective and understand that there are reasons beyond what you might comprehend at the time, you can let go with love. The opposite of love is not hate, it is fear. Too many people go through their life in fear, so they cannot let someone in to love. You cannot have love and fear in your heart at the same time. Many people are so afraid to get hurt they refuse to love. The saying that it is better to have loved and lost than never to have loved at all is very true; it is how your soul grows the fastest. The challenge is to move beyond the hurt and let go with unconditional love so that you can love again.

This love lesson starts with learning how to love yourself unconditionally. You are one of our great Creator's most prized accomplishments, and our Creator does not make mistakes. You are unique in the fact that there is only one of you. Even if you were an identical twin, you would have different characteristics, different quirks, different likes, and a separate soul. Every parent can still tell their identical twins apart, no matter how much they look alike.

You were put here for a very important reason, and you have a purpose. It is your job to figure out the purpose and the real reason that you are here, which, hopefully, you will learn as you go through learning your five love lessons. Some of the reasons are to love always, to learn, to have fun, and to help teach, or help someone else. But you need to discover the specific reason for your life. It is also always about soul growth, yours, and everyone else's. When you are on your life path, everything starts to unfold easily for you, and the answers will be shown to you.

There are people born with physical deformities that have incredible self-esteem, and it becomes infectious to the people around them. You need to always focus on the positive attributes that you have and change the things you do not like, the things that are within your power to change.

We are always a work in progress, and always right where we are supposed to be at any given time. Your journey cannot be rushed, no matter how much you want answers; you have to go through the process. Loving without conditions can be a challenge, whether it is loving yourself or loving another person. Love yourself no matter what you look like, or what you think you did to disappoint yourself or someone else. Love yourself through your mistakes, knowing that you are a work in process, and the next time you will know and do better. Love yourself through your weaknesses and your strengths, knowing you did your best. If there are things that you do not "like" or love about yourself, you have it within your power to change those things, within reason. Love yourself while you are working on that. You should always love yourself, and understand that the challenges you face, are just that—challenges for you to learn how to overcome. Without the challenges, we would live a very boring existence.

Many people have addiction issues, and they feel they are not worthy somehow because of that. It could be alcohol, drugs, sex, or work. For an addict, the addiction itself never goes away, it just changes from one thing to the next. You chose that path before you came here so that you could challenge yourself to channel the addiction into something that is beneficial, not destructive, to you. Do not get caught in the trap people set, trying to make you feel that you are in some way defective or unworthy.

Many people have some form of addiction, whether it is smoking, television, working out, or eating; some addictions are just more stigmatized and advertised than others. There are many ways to channel an addiction into something healthier. Maybe you will become an amazing chef, addicted to learning the most complicated of recipes or creating your own recipes. Maybe you could be addicted to writing and can tell the world the most amazing stories from your life experiences or your imagination. You could turn your addiction to music and want to learn how to write music or play many instruments.

As you can see, addiction is not a bad thing when you look at the positivity that can come out of it. Many discoveries have come about from someone not giving up and turning their addiction into the commitment and staying power to prove that something exists. You just have to find what it is you want to channel your addiction into and then do the work. Some of the most famous people and some of the best inventions known to man were created by someone that channeled their addiction into something productive instead of destructive. You are never given more than you can handle. Believe this, and trust....you created your plan.

Unconditional love also means loving others as they are. Do not expect to love them when they change if you cannot love them the way they are now. Too many people get married to someone thinking that they can make them change into someone else, or that they will change for them after marriage. People change because they have to or they want to, not because someone else wants them to change. Loving and liking are two very different things. You may not "like" what someone is doing or saying, but you can still love them anyway.

Think of all the times your parents reprimanded you as a child. You may have been angry at the punishment and not liked what they said or did, but you still loved them. For those of us who have children, it is the same thing. Even if your child committed a heinous crime and went to prison, you would not like what they did, but you, hopefully, you would still love the child.

We all make mistakes and have bumps to contend with along the road. That is what makes us human; it is ultimately how we learn. We are all imperfectly perfect just the way we are. We are also exactly where we are supposed to be at any given time. Everyone's lesson is to love themselves no matter what, and no matter why they think they are not worthy.

Think of what a boring world it would be if we were all the same. It would be like a bad movie made up of robots. We all also need to learn to embrace the things that make us different and set us apart. We should not let our mistakes define us but realize the fact that we overcame the challenges that have been put before us and the soul growth we gained with wisdom. As long as you always make the best decision with the knowledge you have at hand at the time, and listen to your soul, then you have nothing to feel guilty about. You did what you were supposed to do, and you should stand proud in that knowledge.

A lot of people feel pity for themselves, or for other people, instead of looking at any situation from a higher perspective. When you realize that everyone is actually doing what they are supposed to be doing, to learn or to help, then you can actually see things from a soul level and realize you are watching an interactive movie.

Life is very much like improvisational theater. That is where your choices come in, how will you handle a situation, and what you will choose to do. The Universe always tries to give you a choice. There will always be people who are smarter, prettier, or more skilled than you are. That does not mean that they do not have their own lessons and struggles in their life. It just means they may be different from your lessons. You have no idea what they are struggling with or what their love lessons are.

When you can see things from a higher perspective, you can start being more grateful. That is the beginning of unconditional love. You can love someone even though they have hurt you when you see the lesson that they are, hopefully, learning, or the lesson they were teaching you. It does not mean that you need to continue having that person in your life if they do not bring you joy in some way; it means you can let go with unconditional love and understanding.

Sometimes it is very difficult to see the bigger picture. Especially when there are so many things that happen, that from the outset, it looks like there is no way to find something positive. Even a miscarriage or a child born that only survives a few days happened for a reason. The child's soul chose to only be here for a short time to help someone with their lesson. Maybe the lesson was for the doctor, the nurse, or for one or both of the people involved in making the child. Maybe it was a catalyst for something else or was meant to bring people closer. Possibly, it was a lesson in loving and letting go in a very big way.

Some things seem to make no sense to you at the time, and you may never find the lesson in what happened. If that is the case, it just means the lesson was not meant for you, it was meant for someone else. Nothing in the world that happens is random; everything that happens has a purpose and a reason for happening. Always remember, the answer to any question is love, unconditional love.

Love and gratitude are the two highest vibrations there are. When you are grateful to the Universe for the things that you have, the experiences that you have enjoyed, and the people in your life, you vibrate at a very high vibration. Your energy becomes a magnet for the world, and the Universe will bring you more and more of the things that you desire.

Negativity will lower that vibration; it will flip your magnet over, and push things away—people, experiences, and your own happiness. This is not to say that you have to walk around like Pollyanna, with a smile on your face all the time. We are all human, we have our ups and downs and some disappointments in our lives. You are entitled to have a five-minute "poor me" pity party and then pick yourself back up to carry on with your journey. Be the example you want to set for the rest of the world.

Life is always changing, and the older and wiser you are, the more you have seen, and the more you know that things are always changing. One trauma or drama changes to nothing in no time. Children are at a disadvantage when this comes in because they have not lived long enough to have enough experience to understand the temporary nature of all things. This is why everything that happens to them seems larger than life; they have no context to put things in.

Everyone may not be as fortunate as you are. Maybe they are not as smart or as good-looking. Maybe they have not had the opportunities that you have had in your life. Even if you believe you have not had many, there is always someone who has had less. There is always a person that may seem to have it all together on the outside but they are falling apart on the inside. Kindness costs nothing to give but could make the biggest difference in someone else's life. Whenever you have the opportunity to spread kindness to another person, do so. You will find that it not only raises their vibration, but it will raise yours as well.

What you focus on is not only who you become and what you bring into your life, but it is all the Universe hears. The Universe does not understand negatives. A great example of that is the person trying to cross the street. If they keep saying, "I do not want to get hit by a car, I do not want to get hit by a car," the only thing the Universe hears is "Get hit by a car." They are almost guaranteed to get hit by a car eventually. If they stayed positive instead and said, "I am going to be fine crossing this street," then they will be.

Always remember, thoughts are things they are pure energy, and thus, where your thoughts go, your energy flows. If you constantly have a certain person on your mind all the time, I can guarantee that you are on their mind just as much. Did you ever find that you and someone close to you are having similar thoughts at the same time, and you joke that great minds think alike? It is actually the energy of your thoughts being sent back and forth between you. It is also known as your psychic ability. Did you ever think about someone and they either called you or showed up somewhere in a very short period of time? It is the same energy, and your thoughts are sending it out to the other person.

I was at the book club the other day, and we were all talking about a woman who was not there, and how she had gotten locked in the bathroom the last time she was there. Within minutes she showed up; she had decided to just stop in and get a coffee. All the collective energy literally made her appear. This is why the power of prayer is so strong. You have that collective energy focusing on one primary objective.

There is a doctor by the name of Joe Dispenza, who has been doing peer-reviewed studies for medical journals on the power of group meditation. He is focused on killing cancer cells in people by focusing the energy from the people. He will have terminally ill people allow a group of twelve individuals to meditate over them twenty-four hours a day, for a period of time, focusing all their intentions and collective energy on killing off the cancer cells.

He apparently has completely cured people who were terminally ill with just weeks or months left to live in this manner. He also had them sit around and focus on killing cancer cells that were kept in the frozen medical equipment to keep them from dying, and the collective energy from the meditation raised the temperature of the equipment just enough to kill the cancer cells inside the equipment. He has been able to replicate his findings over and over and have them peer reviewed. You can research him, join his podcasts, and even go to his symposiums, where he does his research using the people in the audience as his test subjects. His ultimate goal is to have health insurances pay for people to have meditation done and include it as a way to heal and cure sicknesses such as cancer.

The friends and lovers you attract into your life are all on that same energetic frequency as you are. Your energy works similarly to a radio station. You cannot get the radio station in if you are not on the right frequency. The people you pull into your life are the same way. They have to be on the same frequency as you. If you want new people to come into your life, you need to raise your vibration.

Laugher is something that can raise your frequency very quickly. It is not as high as love or gratitude, but it's right below the level you want to be on and will help your energy level to rise. You may notice that loving and gratitude toward someone is much easier if you have been laughing together first. If you have not noticed, try it. Tell each other some funny jokes, watch a funny movie together, or go see a comedy show. Anytime you are doing something you truly enjoy, or spending time with someone you want to be with, you are working on raising that vibration, and working toward unconditional love.

Love Lesson 5: Patience

There are many sayings revolving around patience, including "patience is a virtue," and "good things come to those who are patient." Patience can be an extremely difficult love lesson to learn because everyone hates to wait, and we want things to happen when we want them to happen.

We also now live in a culture of instant gratification. We have movies and television shows on demand, instant messaging, and fast food outlets. Everyone carries a cell phone and can be reached and can respond within moments. People have sex on the first date before they have any idea with whom they are having sex, and they have children before they even decide if the person that is bringing a child into this world with them is someone that they even want in their life, so they get married later instead of first.

Sometimes it seems like the whole world has lost the entire meaning of the word patience. We have no control over the timing of things in our life, our higher self; the part of our soul that is in the fifth dimension controls that. In fact, time only exists here on Earth, not anywhere else in the Universe. We created time in order to try to have the illusion of controlling things that we really cannot control. It can be very unnerving if you think about the fact that there are lots of happenings out of your control. The fact that the whole game could end by the pressing of a button and a nuclear war could happen at any time, is enough to put some people completely over the edge!

The reason that people set alarm clocks and have routines that they repeat over and over, is to feel like they have some control in this world. The routine itself gives them some kind of stability and peace. The fact remains, the only control you have is your reaction to things and the decisions that you make in the situations that are presented to you by the Universe.

It can be very difficult to wait for something when you want it so badly. Especially when we allow ourselves to look at the limited time we are really on the earth. We have a short span of time to accomplish many things. This is the reason that older people started compiling what is called a "bucket list." This is a list of things they want to accomplish before "kicking the bucket," so to speak.

Suppose you wanted to get married and have a family and you are worried because you are not as young as you used to be, and your so-called biological clock is ticking away. If it was written into your plan, it will happen, most likely when you least expect it. You may have written a different plan for yourself, however. Maybe you will marry a widow or widower later in life and help them raise their family. Maybe you will help raise a family member's children after something unexpected happens. Maybe it was not something that you chose to happen this time around for any number of different reasons. Maybe that scenario tied you down too much in a previous lifetime, and you decided that in this lifetime, you wanted more freedom.

All you can do is put the intention out to the Universe that there is something you want and see if you can magnetize it into your life. If it is meant to be, it will be when the timing is right and you are ready. Otherwise, enjoy what the Universe brings you, and stop questioning the timing and the reason why.

When your vibration is high, the things you want will come to you much faster. I remember asking the Universe to help me buy a new car. When covid hit, I had time on my hands and decided to look for a newer car. My car was already four years old, and I was used to replacing it every two to three years. I wanted a BMW diesel like I had leased a few years earlier, midnight blue metallic with saddle brown tan interior. I discovered that the last year they were allowed to import diesel vehicles into the United States was 2018, due to the new emission standards. The new "green deal" was already kicking in even back then. I figured I would have to buy a used one, which would still be an upgrade to my 2015 model. All the used ones I was finding were colors I did not like, black on black, and white on white, with thirty–thousand miles on them. They were all about $40,000 used.

I meditated and asked the angels for help in finding me the best car that they could. Within a few hours, I received an email from a dealership in another state, not anyone that I had contacted. They had the exact car I wanted, midnight blue metallic with saddle brown tan interior, brand new on the showroom floor as a leftover, with no miles, full warranty, and the same price as a used one—$40.000.

Obviously, this was supposed to be my car; they would not have found it for me otherwise. I filled out the loan application for it and was quickly denied, due to a recent divorce and bankruptcy. I again meditated and talked to the angels. I said that they obviously wanted me to have this car, or they would not have sent it, and now they needed to help me find a way to pay for it since I could not get the loan.

Within the next few days, enough people had joined my Relationship Mastery Program and paid up front, that I had money to buy the car and have it delivered. Even though I know how it all works, and I teach other people how to attract into their life what they want and need, I still get very excited and very grateful when I do it for myself, with the Universe's help.

Amazing things happen when your vibration is high. You turn into a powerful magnet of energy. If you ask the Universe to bring you something, or for something specific to happen, rest assured, from your mouth to their ears! They begin working on it right away, but the timing of the event is in play, as well as it being for your highest and best.

This is where patience really comes in. If it is brought to you too early, you may not be ready, and you may not appreciate it. If it is brought to you too late in life, you would most likely lose out on a lot of the experiences. If you are asking the Universe to bring you a specific person, however, a lot of patience will be needed. If it is a specific person you are asking for, they have their plan and lessons as well, which have to sync up to your timing and vibration. This also speaks to the lesson of trust, because once you have asked the Universe for someone, you need to trust that the Universe will bring them for you, just not necessarily in the timeframe you were hoping for. Everything comes when it is supposed to, teaching you your lesson in patience.

Staying in the *now* helps you to learn all the love lessons a lot easier. If you keep hoping for the future, you will end up living in a state of constant anxiety. If you keep dwelling on the past, you live in a perpetual state of regret, and possibly sorrow, lowering your energetic vibration. *Now* is the only thing that really exists because no one knows when their last today is. What is happening today? What decisions can you make that may change the direction of not only your life but someone else's life? This is where you need to keep your focus and concentrate on all the positive things you can find each day. This will give you more peace and happiness in your life—in the *now*—and give you the patience to weather the unknown future. Before you know it, the future, and things better than what you could have imagined, will have arrived.

How Do We Connect With Our Soul?

It is not as difficult as you think to connect with your soul; you just have to learn how to listen. Your soul, and the souls of those that have passed before you, are always trying to send you messages and help you. The easiest way to start connecting with your soul is through meditation. I know what your next thought is; "There's no way I can meditate"! I once thought the same thing as well.

I was going through a second divorce that was dragging on to its second year, my sister was dying, and I was having a lot of trouble in my businesses because the economy was terrible. I was having a hard time finding enough help to operate properly, and I was hiring people even though my "gut instinct" told me I should not. I felt that I had to hire them so I would literally have the body since I was short-staffed. I was making decisions out of desperation.

I had also met my twin flame during this time, and my head was literally spinning. He was going through his own upheaval in his personal life and did not want to see me, and he could not quite explain why. I think he was experiencing fear from the connection we had since it was so intense. I had no idea why meeting him and being around him affected me so much. The first sexual experience we had together literally projected me back into the fifth dimension, just like when I had died.

I later learned that is what the kundalini awakening is. It was the catalyst for my spiritual awakening and to putting me on the path of helping others. I never told him, but the last time we were together in that way, I knew in my soul that it would be the last time for a long time. I cried quietly all night long. I had never had that feeling with anyone else in my life. It was the most peaceful experience—like I was home. I felt like I had found the person I had looked for my whole life—like he was a part of me. The feeling I had and still have, is not really even explainable in words, it goes much deeper, into my soul.

I went to see a Reiki practitioner to see if she could help me relax and explain why I could not seem to get someone I dated out of my head, my heart, and my soul. I certainly had never heard the term "twin flame" before. After doing some Reiki, she told me I needed to learn how to meditate to relax. Of course, I did not think it was something I would be able to do. I could not stop the million things running around in my head. The businesses I was running, the divorce I was going through, and the feelings I had for "this guy." The first time I meditated, my psychic abilities and mediumship abilities came back to me in full force. It was because I was getting in touch with my soul and out of my computer head. Overthinking is a problem for a lot of people. It does not usually help a situation; it just makes you obsess over it. The Universe knew the timing, and this was apparently the time.

Even when you think you are not meditating properly or enough, you are connecting to the other side and your soul. It may only be for a few minutes when you first start, but the effects are cumulative. The more often you meditate, the easier it becomes, the faster you connect, and the stronger you connect with your soul and the other side. You also start connecting faster the more you meditate and for longer periods of time. Meditation also raises your vibration and gives you more energy.

Think of it as plugging an extension cord into the wall and recharging your body. The results of meditating on a regular basis are amazing. Since you are speeding up the molecules in your body, your cells turn over faster, thus, you turn the clock back and start looking younger. That in itself is a reason everyone should start meditating!

You will also find that your body requires less sleep. I used to need an eight-hour night's sleep or I could not properly function the next day. If I was overly stressed,

I would need a solid nine hours of sleep. Now, I need six hours, and I have not used an alarm clock to get up in the morning in many years. That is unless I need to catch a plane, but I find even then I still get up before the alarm. You may feel that your body temperature is a little higher as well, or you get frequent hot flashes. That is because the energy makes the molecules in your body speed up, making you feel warmer.

When I channel souls through from the other side at shows on a stage, I almost feel like my body is going to catch fire. Meditation also helps to relieve anxiety, stress, sleep disorders, and post-traumatic stress disorder and gives you an all-around sense of calm and peace. This is the soul connection that you are making. When we pray, we are asking a higher conscience—or the Universe—and a higher power for something that we either want or want an answer to. When we meditate, we get the answers to what we asked.

You may see faces when you meditate, bright lights, or shapes. Relatives and friends that have passed may just show up in your head as a thought or show you something to see. Even messages from people who are living may pop into your head. There is nothing to be concerned with; as long as you have protected yourself, nothing evil can contact you. You can also ask questions while you are meditating. If something pops into your head, you know it is coming from the other side, not from you. If your mind starts to wander to grocery shopping, or some mundane tasks you have to do like laundry, just move those thoughts on. If you do not get your answer right away, it will come to you later, like when you are driving or just doing some other activity. It will just pop into your head, seemingly out of nowhere.

You also have a special guide that is there with you always. He is known as your gatekeeper. He stays with you throughout your life and will take direction from you in regard to who and what you want to talk to and see, or what you don't want to see when you're meditating and connecting to the other side. You are always the one in control.

My gatekeeper is a Native American Indian and has only spoken to me twice. I have also only seen his face twice, even though I sense him always standing behind my right shoulder. You can give your gatekeeper any directions that you want because you are always in charge. You can always ask for your gatekeeper to introduce themselves to you during meditation, and even ask their name. Usually, they are more than happy to show themselves.

When I do mediumship at large events, my gatekeeper is the one that lines the souls up on the other side, so when I go to a certain person in the audience, he makes sure the right soul for that person is next in line. We also have a few understandings between us from the directions I have given him. If I need to see how someone died, I do not want to see any blood or gore; I am not sure I could handle it. They can show me everything else without having to include that detail. If I am not actually working, he does not allow souls to come and bother me; he keeps them at bay. They are actually everywhere. The exception to that is if there is an emergency.

I once had a friend, who had passed away about six months previously, show up in my shower with me. I asked her what was wrong, and she told me that her husband was so depressed that he was going to commit suicide. I was leaving that morning to go out of town for a few days, and I knew I had no time to go visit him because he lived about forty-five minutes away. I called to check on him and prayed for Archangel Michael to watch over him until I returned on the following Monday.

The first thing I did when I got back was to go to his home. I let him know that his wife had come to see me and said she was afraid he was going to try to commit suicide. He broke down in tears and told me that she had also gone to visit his brother and had told him the very same thing. He said he just missed her so much and did not know what his purpose was here anymore without her. We talked and discovered a few things to keep him busy and bring joy into his life, including adopting an older dog for company and spending more time with his grandchildren. He also realized that he was still needed here for his children and that he had things that he still needed to do here on Earth.

The only other time a soul came through in an emergency was when a friend's fiancé had just passed away. He had been in the Massachusetts Hospital in ICU with pneumonia and was expected to make a full recovery. My girlfriend left him in the hospital with full confidence that he would be fine and drove back to New Hampshire, two states away, to go back to work.

He came to me, not realizing he was dead, and could not understand why he could not get back into his body. His soul went to see my girlfriend at her job because he missed her, and when his soul had left his body, his body had expired. He thought he had done something wrong and he did not understand the reason that he could not get back into his body. He had obviously gone into the light, however, or he would not have been able to travel to see me.

The majority of your soul can leave your body when you are sleeping in deep meditation, under medical care, in certain emergencies, and when your body is dying. There is always a small part of your soul left behind to maintain the body and keep you alive. If the body cannot be maintained that small part of your soul that had remained in your body joins the rest of your soul. Some of it is stored in the fifth dimension and orchestrates the timing for the events happening here. The rest, known as your aura, is hovering over your body.

Once he understood that he had passed away and had actually gone into the light and returned, he wanted to be with her when she heard the news. I did not feel that I should be the person to tell her he had passed away; I did not feel that it was my place to do so. I waited until that evening to call and see how she was doing, and she let me know he had passed away. I let her know at the funeral that when she was ready there were some things I needed to tell her and that he had come to visit me. It took her over a year to finally be ready to hear what happened that day. Now they are in contact on a regular basis since she knows how to read the signs he gives.

How To Meditate

To begin your meditation, make sure that you are wearing comfortable clothing and find a time and place where you will not be interrupted. You want to limit yourself to twenty-minute sessions when you are just starting out with meditation. I would recommend starting twice a day and then doing three times a day after you are comfortable with the process. If you meditate any longer than twenty minutes, your body starts to become ungrounded.

What does it mean to become ungrounded? It means that after the meditation, you will be walking around like you have your head in the clouds, like an "airhead," forgetting everything you need to do in the "3D" world. If you want to take some classes on guided meditations that last longer or do them yourself after you are proficient in meditation, that is fine, but you first need to learn the basics and get in touch with your soul.

I was making meatballs one day and realized they needed another fifteen minutes in the oven. I figured I would take the opportunity to meditate for a few minutes and connect to the other side; however, I neglected to set a timer for myself. I got into such a deep meditation that forty-five minutes went by before I came out of it. I then started going about my daily chores. I went upstairs and got a load of laundry together, and when I came back down, I noticed that I had forgotten to shut the oven off after I made the meatballs. Then it dawned on me that I had never taken the meatballs out of the oven! Needless to say, they were quite shriveled up and burnt at that point. This is an example of the things that can happen if you are not grounded properly.

Find yourself a chair that you can sit upright in and keep both your feet on the floor. This helps with the grounding. I like to play some soft new-age type music in the background; I just make sure the vibration of the music is above 528MZ. Believe it or not, all the music you listen to on the radio is below 528mz. It was decided worldwide around 1950 to keep all the music you listen to at 440MZ. It is technically a lower vibration and that keeps you depressed. Even an upbeat tune is at a lower energetic vibration.

You may have to search for the music by vibration on a music channel, YouTube, Pandora, or Rumble. I like to listen to music in the 900 range or above. You can set the mood for yourself any way you need to when you are starting out. You can lower the lighting, light a candle, burn incense, whatever you want. The better you get at meditation, and the more you do it, the less you will need the props. I do not recommend it, but I have been known to meditate even when driving with my eyes open. At that point, it is all about the connection with the other side, which I can do now in seconds. The more you meditate, the faster you will connect to your soul.

Sit comfortably in the chair, with your feet on the ground, and picture yourself as a tree. Picture yourself with roots growing out of your feet, growing all the way down into the ground and deep into the earth. Picture the roots growing all the way down into the center of the earth to keep you grounded there. Keep your hands in a comfortable position in front of you but not crossed over you.

That is a protective stance; you want to show that you are open. You may want to have your palms up in your lap if it is comfortable for you. Take a few deep breaths through your nose and release the air slowly through your mouth. After you recite the following prayer for meditation, close your eyes, and try to focus on the pinpoint of light that you will see. Make sure to always recite the meditation prayer the same way, every time, unless you are asking for someone specific to come in and visit with you, and then add their name. Always ask Archangel Michael for protection. This is where some people get into trouble. When you open yourself up for good, you also open yourself up for evil. Again, just because you cannot see them, it does not mean they are not there. Anyone with a good heart is a target for evil in this world. You always need to ask for protection from the angels. If you do not ask, they cannot jump in to protect you, no matter how much they want to.

There are many rules on the other side; this is just one of them. Now, literally, read out loud the following prayer, until you can say it from memory.

Please let me sit on the power of love and light. I ask my angels, guides, archangels, ascended masters, loved ones, and any other higher vibrational entities that want to come in and be with me to come in. Please give me messages and information from the other side that is clear, concise, verifiable, evidentiary, detailed, and for my highest and best. (If there is anything specific you need, like a name or a detail, you can add that and ask as well.) *Archangel Michael, please surround me with love and light, and protect me from any lower vibrational entities, any attachments, and any harm. Please protect my loved ones, and my loved ones, loved ones.*

If there is anyone specific you want to connect with, call them by name for their soul to be with you as well. When you pray, you are asking for something; when you meditate, you are receiving your answers. Prayers work, because of the energetic cadence that is created when they are said. If you have ever been to a Catholic

Church service, you will notice that the priest actually sounds like he is half-singing some of the prayers.

The Hierarchy Of The Other Side

Whatever you want to call it, there is only one "source energy." You can call it God, Mohamed, Krishna, Allah, Jehovah, Brahman, Yahweh, etc., it really does not matter what the name is. When you get there, you will realize they are all one and the same.

There are several different levels of heaven that we can go to, however. It was explained to me that it is similar to a layer cake. We go to the level or dimension of heaven that is connected to our soul growth. Our belief system is directly related to our soul growth because we do not fully understand something unless we have experienced it.

This is the difference between knowledge and wisdom. Therefore, the souls with the same belief systems and the souls with the same level of growth reside on the same levels. I really have no idea how many levels there are, it is not an answer I have been able to get yet. I also do not know how new souls are formed either, other than a soul splitting into two during the twin flame process. There are many questions and many things still to learn about the other side. They seem to give out the information on an as-needed basis. The education from the other side seems to be very systematic and amazing, however. They have taught me things I never could have imagined!

My mom died one year to the day that my dad died, December twenty-first, and at the same age, ninety-three. Even though they had not been married or together for over fifty years, they stayed in touch and talked on the phone together every day, until my mother had an epiphany in the nursing home. She suddenly realized one day that he had been an abusive husband and that she deserved better. At that moment, she understood her self-worth. She decided she did not want to talk to him anymore and did not do so for the remainder of their lives. It just goes to show, you are never too old to learn your love lessons.

My mom was also a medium, although I never knew until later in life because she did not raise me. I ended up training at some of the same places she had trained fifty years earlier. There were still a few old-timers there who remembered her.

When they brought my mom up to the hospital room from the emergency department, there was an angel sitting right next to the television set above the shelf. I asked my mom at the time if she saw him, and she said no. During the night, I asked the angel what his name was. He said it was Makael, not Michael, although they are apparently the same angel. I looked up his name,

Makael, the next day after my mom passed, and it said he was the angel that brings advanced souls to the higher realms upon their death. Had he told me his name was Michael, I would not have looked it up, since I know he is also the angel of protection.

They are always teaching from the other side if you pay attention to the lesson. My mom was escorted to the other side by multiple family members and the angel, Makael. She immediately went to my deceased father's side, who thanked her for coming through in this lifetime to help him learn whatever it was he was working on learning. As much as I do this work, and I know what I know, it was still a stunning sight for me to watch. I thought he would have been the last person she would have wanted to see on the other side. Another lesson was reinforced for me and for them: unconditional love.

Angels are their own race of beings. They were never human beings, and there are millions of them. They exist only to help us; it is what gives them purpose. In order to help us though, they need to be asked. If you do not ask, they cannot help. Apparently, it is one of the required rules. There are rules on the other side, just as there are rules here. Everyone also has things to do. It is one of the ways all souls, here and on the other side, feel fulfilled and have a sense of accomplishment. It is the same thing in both places; the more you accomplish the more gratified you feel. Souls do get to enjoy the other side and can go wherever they want, but they still need to work on learning their lessons on the other side, the same as they had to work on learning them when they were here.

When I first started my work, I did not think I was worthy of calling on an archangel like Michael to protect me before I meditated. I also did not understand the extent that evil will go to when it wants to try and infiltrate someone's life. I thought Michael must be very busy and have more important things to do than to protect little old me. It was explained to me from the other side that just like when we go into the light and we suddenly have no body, and we have the power to travel anywhere in an instant, they can do the same. Angels can help and protect millions of people in the blink of an eye. Everyone is worthy and should not hesitate to ask for help.

The first angel that I ever channeled was one of the nine choir angels that sits at the side of the Almighty. The choir angels are known to sing all day and sit at the right hand of God, according to the Bible. Apparently, they also have other things that they do. The first angel that ever came through for me to see was a choir angel.

I was doing Reiki work on a client who came into my business. She was a young girl whom I had never seen before. I had only one other person that was also a

Reiki practitioner in my business, and since she was busy, the appointment was scheduled for me. While I was in the middle of the session, the room started to fill with light from the ceiling at the head of the bed. The light was blinding, but the all-familiar feeling I had when I had died had come back. I was awash in the feeling of love, and peace. It was more than just being in love; it was being bathed in love all around me. I dropped to my knees on the side of the table and tears of joy started rolling down my face.

The angel said she was Seraphiel, and that she wanted the girl to know that her child was going to do great things for humanity. She wanted the mother not to worry or have any fear and know that she was protecting her and her child. Then the angel left. I was grateful for the fact that the girl had her eyes closed on the table, and had no idea I was on the floor, on my knees, crying.

When the session was over, I asked her how she was feeling and if she wanted to know what happened. She said that she did, so I recanted what the angel had said about protecting her and her child, and what the angel's name was. Not having grown up in any one particular religion, I had no idea if the name was real, or something I may have heard wrong. I was also fairly new to understanding all of my gifts and practicing Reiki. The girl started to cry and said that this was the first time she had been out of the house without her child. She said she had a little boy who was over a year old, and she was afraid to leave him with anyone. She was afraid something might happen to him if she was not there. She was grateful for the information and felt more at peace knowing she was protected.

After she left, I looked up the name of the angel on my phone. I was shocked when it came up as one of the highest choir angels. It is always nice to have things confirmed and know that you are not crazy. I ran out to the parking lot to show her it was real and caught her right before she pulled out. I was still trying to wrap my own head around it, since having a choir angel appear in front of me. was such an intense experience.

After the choir angels are the archangels. There are seven archangels, and each archangel is in charge of a soul group. These are the people that you reincarnate with lifetime after lifetime. There are millions of souls in each soul group. Before you can reincarnate, they must make sure you are actually ready to come back. You meet with the archangels and the other souls you are going to reincarnate with to make your plan. It is almost like making up your own board game. You choose whom you will interact with and all the events that will occur during your lifetime here. Even though we come back for multiple reasons, your plan is very complicated.

Think about how many people you interact with on a daily or weekly basis. Believe it or not, just saying something nice to the girl at the coffee shop or the restaurant might change their mind as to whether or not they keep the job they are in, move, or even decide not to take their own life. All of these interactions have been written into your life plan. We all are very powerful beings, and what we do and say, and the energy we put out to the world, all make a difference.

You need to decide whom you are going to help with what love lessons and what you need to learn while you are here. You also have to look at whom you owe karma to and who owes you from a past lifetime. You all chose and agree to come back together and to interact when the time comes, so it all works like an orchestrated interactive play. I say interactive because we have free will to a point. You can choose to delay your love lessons that you came here to learn, but you cannot change the fact that you need to learn them all. We like to think that we have choices, but your choices will always bring you back in a circle if it is not the right choice.

Let us compare it to a game show. You get to choose from doors number one, two, or three. You choose door number one, and you go through. On the other side of the door, you get married, have a few children, buy a house, and get divorced. You take the long walk around and end up in front of doors one, two, and three again. If you have not learned your love lesson, you will take door one again. Guess what? Beyond door one, you will get married, have children, and buy a house again. Then you will get divorced for the second time. Once you take the long walk back to the doors, if you still have not learned, you will continue to take door one. If you have learned what you were supposed to learn, you will choose another door. Not to say you may not get married again through that door, but it will not end it divorce because you learned the love lesson you needed to learn. Not to say everyone is on the path of marriage, but whatever it is you are doing and not learning is what you are repeating and keeping you from being on the path you belong on.

Archangels are very powerful beings; this is why we call upon them to help protect us, to heal us, etc. They also all have different specialties.

We already know Archangel Michael is whom you call on for protection; Archangel Raphael can be called on for healing and works very closely with Mother Mary, whom you can also ask. Archangel Gabriel is the angel of communication; you can call on him when you really need to hear from someone. Archangel Jophiel is responsible for directing your attention back to love, to help you learn the lesson of unconditional love. Archangel Ariel is responsible for protecting the earth and all of its inhabitants. Archangel Azrael helps the diseased transition when they pass, and Archangel Chamuel is responsible for bringing peace to the earth and also helping twin flame souls to reconnect. Archangel Metatron is also responsible for re-connecting twin flame souls and is responsible for guarding the secrets of heaven.

There are more archangels, but these are the ones that we commonly work with and see more often on Earth.

Then there are lower-level angels that are sent randomly to help and intervene. People often comment about someone being an angel on Earth and angels on Earth actually do appear to intervene when they are really needed.

I remember many years ago, after I had my second child, I was experiencing post-partum depression. I am not sure that they were very familiar with the condition at the time or what the cause was, but I remember experiencing a lot of highs and lows after his birth. I contacted the ob-gyn at the time and explained to the nurse practitioner how I was feeling and what was happening. Instead of making an appointment for me, she asked me if I had ever seen a psychiatrist and said that maybe I needed one. That was not the answer I was looking for. I knew it was some kind of a hormone imbalance I was having from delivering the baby. I felt deflated and did not know what to do next.

Back then, I was going to the gym on a regular basis to walk the one-mile track and lose the excess baby weight I had put on. I remember walking down the hallway to the showers when I was literally stopped by a woman coming around the corner. She looked at me and asked if everything was all right. Here she is, a perfect stranger, and I start unloading on her about how I recently had a baby and I was having a lot of mood swings and depression. I told her what the nurse had said, and that I felt lost. She handed me a business card and said I should call her primary care doctor, that she would be able to help me. I took the card, thanked her, and then started walking toward the showers again.

I realized I never got her name, so I turned around to ask her, and she was gone. There is no way she could have gotten to the end of the hallway that fast. I have no explanation as to where she went, and really thought it was odd that she just happened to have her doctor's business card ready to hand out.

I realized sometime much later that she was an earth angel. Another interesting fact that I learned is that if you should encounter an earth angel, their feet never touch the earth. I did not know it at the time or have the presence of mind to notice. Her doctor was unable to take me, but the new doctor in the office did. She treated me for the hormone imbalance and was truly one of the best doctors I ever had the pleasure of being a patient of. I was with her from the time she graduated medical school until she passed at the young age of forty-five from breast cancer.

Different angels hang around us a good part of the time, waiting to be asked to help. I often see angels directly above or behind people when I am standing there and having a conversation with them. You can always ask the angels for help with little things, like finding a parking spot or looking for an item in the grocery store, etc. They will happily direct you and are grateful for the opportunity to help since it gives them purpose.

Then there is what everyone likes to call their guardian angel. Guardian angels are not actually angels at all. When you are born, all the souls that have been related or connected to your soul for the past few centuries are asked who would like to be your guardian angel. Maybe you remind another soul of what they looked like or acted like when they were here, and someone agrees to step up and do the job. If none of them step up, because they just are not interested, one is chosen.

Your guardian angel can also change during your lifetime. If you had someone pass in this lifetime, and they had a very strong connection with you—maybe a best friend, a lover, or a relative—they can ask to be your guardian angel when they get to the other side. When that happens, the original guardian angel hangs back and supervises the one that just took over. So technically, you have two guardian angels at one time. Guardian angels do not need to be asked to step in and help you, although you can absolutely ask if you want help.

Many times, you have no idea how the guardian angel is connected to you, or who they are. If you find yourself in a dangerous situation, your guardian angel will step in without you asking for help, unlike an actual angel. Let us say, for instance, that you were driving your car on an icy road and lost control of the steering. Somehow, it seemed like someone or something else literally grabbed the wheel and steered you to safety. That somebody would have been your guardian angel. They are always around you and always looking for ways to help and protect you. Everyone on the other side wants you to succeed on your visit here.

Angels are always trying to connect with you to help you get on the life path you came here for and to encourage you. Angels only talk in binary code and numbers, however. In order to understand what they want to tell you, you need to learn their language.

The foremost authority on angel numbers was Doreen Virtue, Ph.D. I say *was* because even though she studied the angels and the meaning of the different numbers for years, her path brought her to marry a very religious Catholic man, who believed she was talking to demons. She has since written another book of numbers, not spiritual, that does not resonate with most people I know who work with angels. The original book is out of print but can still be found on eBay and other used book sites. The title is *Angel Numbers*, by Doreen Virtue, Ph.D., and Lynette Brown. Make sure that anytime you look up anything online, you put "spiritual" in the front so you get the correct answers.

Have you ever noticed that you keep seeing the same repeating numbers going on? That is because they want to give you a message, and they are trying to get your attention. Have you ever noticed you keep catching the clock at 11:11 or 1:11 all the time? That is the angels letting you know they are nearby you, and they hear what you want and need. Have you ever woken up at night at the same time night after night? Maybe it is 1:11 or 3:33? 3:33 is the number of the ascended masters. That means you have their attention, and you have the ascended masters working on your issues for you. These are usually the first signs that your soul is ready for a spiritual awakening to occur in your life and put you on the true path of why you are here.

I remember sitting in traffic once, thinking that I had not gotten any messages recently, feeling that maybe they had forgotten about me. I started to look around, and the license plate on the car in front of me had my initials on it. The telephone pole to the left of me was numbered 5656, which comes to 1111 if you split them and add them up, and the mailbox number to my right was 222. I had not moved an inch in the traffic. Apparently, they were sending me messages everywhere; I just was not paying attention.

Ascended Masters/ Saints/Guides

These all fall into the same category because they were all once human beings on Earth. Ascended masters are the highest level of teachers that have evolved to the highest levels, spiritually. Jesus, Buddha, Mother Mary, Saint Francis, Saint Anthony, Vishnu, Saint Germaine, and the list goes on. You can call on them and they will come to you to help with whatever problems or questions you have.

When I was young, I used to see people driving around with little statues of Mother Mary or Jesus in their cars and think it was ridiculous. I was one of those people who, if I could not touch it, see it, or hear it, it could not be real. I now keep Archangel Michael in my car for protection when I drive, as well as a rosary that was blessed that I received as a gift.

Any time my faith gets shaken even a little, Saint Anthony likes to play games with me. I will lose something important, and he will make it show up after I have looked everywhere for it. Finally, I will sit down and ask him to help me find it, and within a short period of time, sometimes just minutes, I will locate the missing item. The place to look, even if I have already looked, will just pop into my head! Yes, they all seem to have a sense of humor.

One winter I was staying at an Airbnb in Florida for a month. It was just a small one-bedroom unit with a bathroom and an open-air kitchen. I was going golfing with some friends and was running late to the golf course. By the time I got there, I had to grab a golf cart and meet them since they had already teed off at the first hole. Usually, the cart number gets written down by the ranger but I skipped it being in such a hurry. On the second or third hole, it was so windy my hat got blown off of my head but it caught on my earrings, so I put it back on.

When we finished golfing, we met at the nineteenth hole for a quick drink. I am in the habit of always checking my earrings backs on a very expensive pair of diamond earrings my ex-husband had given me. Although I thought I did this multiple times a day, apparently, it was not as often as I thought. I checked my ears and realized one earring was missing. I could not believe it. I looked around the floor and retraced my steps into the building. I went outside to check the golf cart, but without the number, I did not even know what cart it was. I thought for sure the earring must have come off when my hat had blown off and got caught in my earrings.

I went home a little deflated, hoping maybe it had fallen off in my bed in my haste that morning, and I had not noticed I was not wearing it. I went back to the little apartment and tore the whole thing apart, top to bottom. I found absolutely nothing. That night, before I went to bed, I prayed to Saint Anthony. I told him that the earring was not going to change my life in any direction, and I understood if someone who might need it for an engagement ring was supposed to find it on the golf course. I let him know, however, how much I enjoyed wearing the earrings, and what a good memory it brings back to me from my ex-husband. Then I went to bed.

When I got up to go to the bathroom in the morning, I was sitting on the toilet, and for some reason, I looked all the way under it. Right against the bottom of the bowl was my earring. I found the back to it all the way across the room on the floor. This has happened over and over again every time I lose something. I ask, even though some things seem to be a lost cause, and Saint Anthony always comes through and helps me find the missing item.

Whenever I do not feel well, I ask Saint Raphael and Mother Mary to come to heal me. They work together, and I either recover much faster, or I do not get sick at all. I have had to have biopsies done on my thyroid every year for several years, due to nodules and hyperthyroidism. They do not use anesthesia, since it is just a needle extraction, but they are always doing multiple extractions. I call on Mother Mary and Saint Raphael before they begin, and I do not feel a thing through the whole procedure.

Just as the angels send you messages in binary codes and numbers, the ascended masters and guides send you messages as well. Anything that you see that seems to be out of the ordinary is a message from the other side. If you ever have to ask if it is a message, it is. Just like thinking you know who sent the message; your first thought is usually the correct one.

You might see a flock of turkeys fly across the road in front of you or see a turtle walking in your driveway. Look up the spiritual meaning of what you see. There will be several spiritual meanings for the sign. Whatever resonates with you is the message for you. Maybe you see a certain bird everywhere you look. If you cannot identify the type of bird, look up the spiritual meaning of the color of the bird. If you can identify it as a crow, a hawk, or something else, look up the spiritual meaning of that specific bird. I think you'll be pleasantly surprised by how they know what is going on in your life, and how the messages they send connect.

I have a friend whose girlfriend passed away about eight years ago. She always sends him a female cardinal when she is missing him. The cardinal will literally tap on the glass of his kitchen window until he acknowledges the message from her. This has gone on for eight years now, every few months, even in the wintertime with the snow. My mom sends a red-shouldered hawk to my sister, so she knows she is around and thinking about her. My other friend recently had a poisonous snake approach her multiple days in a row. The spiritual message was not only amazing but spot on for what was happening in her life at that moment.

If you ask a question when you are meditating and you do not literally hear the answer as words when you are meditating, they will send it to you in symbols. As a medium, even my loved ones on the other side will frequently communicate with me using symbols. They taught me a whole list of symbols that they use to get the message across if they are not very talkative. These have meaning only to me. They will teach you as well if it is something you feel the calling to pursue. If you feel they sent you a symbol as a message and you do not know the meaning, look it up for yourself to get the answer.

Everything Happens According To The Plan

Know that there are no coincidences in life. Everything that happens to you in your lifetime happens for a reason. You may learn the reason quickly, or it may take some time to determine what the reason was unless it was happening as a lesson for someone else. If you can create a relationship with your own soul and learn how to include the angels and the Universe into your life, you'll understand the why behind the things that are happening to you and around you.

I can remember when I was dating I met a lawyer who seemed to click with me very well. It took me a few weeks to realize he had not been honest with me and was, in fact, still married, and had not even filed for a divorce as he told me he had. I informed him that I did not want to see him any longer but we parted as friends. Fast-forward about six months in time, when I had relocated to Florida and I was buying a new home to live in.

This was around the time that houses were selling at ridiculous prices over the asking price and even over the appraised value. I had what I thought was an iron-clad contract on the purchase price; however, the seller thought he could just back out of the contract and accept a higher cash offer. He thought that by not supplying information for the mortgage company to complete the loan, I would be in default. Had he done that, I would have had no recourse other than to sue him in court and hold the sale of the house up for everyone. This would not only have taken years to meander through the court system but would have also cost me thousands in upfront legal costs.

This all happened on a Friday afternoon, and the contract covenant would have expired at the close of business that day, making it much more difficult to enforce the contract. I contacted at least five real estate attorneys that day, none of whom were able to help with such short notice.

As a last-ditch effort, I contacted the lawyer I had dated months earlier, who had been married. Lo and behold, he spent the entire afternoon putting a letter together for me to send to the seller's real estate agent. It was very strongly worded, spelling out the consequences for not following through with their part of the agreement. The sale went through right after. Had I not met this lawyer a few months earlier, I am sure the sale of the house would not have gone through the way it was supposed to. I realized then what the reason was that we had met because I knew I was meant to own the home that I bought.

I am sure if you look back, you can follow some of the breadcrumbs in your own life and see how one event led to the next and the next, to take you to where you are today. Whenever you are asking yourself why something is happening, or "Why me?' ask instead, "Why not me?" What is the reason or the lesson I am supposed to be getting from this experience?

Is There A Way To Learn All My Lessons In This Lifetime?

The short answer is yes if that is your life path. Even if you do not learn them all in this lifetime, which I do believe is possible, you can learn the majority of your lessons and live an amazing life full of joy, happiness, and amazing possibilities. In order for that to happen, however, you first need to learn how to shift and balance your energy. This is not an easy thing to do, or everyone would not only be doing it, everyone would also be sharing and teaching it. Even the people that I have found teaching the law of attraction do not teach you how to balance your energy. That is why people can make the energy shift and start attracting things into their lives, but they cannot maintain it. It only lasts for a short period of time, and then they go back to the level of vibration they were at prior.

Studies have shown that you can make or break any habit, good or bad, and learn any technique in as little as six weeks. Most people do not realize that it is not only possible but it is not very difficult. If you wanted to quit smoking cigarettes and you found the right program and did the program every day for six weeks, you could quit smoking for the rest of your life. The reason this happens is that your brain is being retrained and rewired. Stronger than any physical addiction is the mental addiction that people have. If you really enjoy smoking, it is harder for you to quit smoking than just having a physical addiction to nicotine. You have to find something that you enjoy as much, if not more, for your brain to rewire itself.

Years ago, I created a seven-week program to teach people how to shift and balance their energy, and to explain how energy and the Universe really work. Why is it a seven-week program instead of six? Because it is a fully comprehensive program that covers all of the different aspects of your life. It touches on marriage, divorce, death, retirement, children, and blended families. I teach you how to talk to the angels and your loved ones, and how to understand and receive the answers.

I still market the program, but mostly to people going through the crisis of separation or divorce. Most people have to be in a crisis situation before they value the information and are willing to do the work in the program that has to be done to make a change. When faced with losing someone you truly love, possibly losing your children, your home, and your lifestyle, the average person is more than willing to do the work to fix the situation. Otherwise, I find that people want the results but they are too lazy to do all the work to get there. My program only works if it is done in order, and in a timely manner. There are no quick fixes in life. If you want the Universe to give you the rewards you desire, you have to first deserve it by doing the work. Then if you are supposed to be back together with the person who was the reason for doing the program, not only do you reunite, but it ends up being a more amazing relationship than you could ever have imagined. Usually, once reunited, the other person is so interested in the reason for the change that they also learn the program through the person that just finished it.

I have students that have taught their children so that they can avoid some of the challenges they would have experienced otherwise. The Universe is not concerned with how you learn your five love lessons, only that you do.

The result of shifting and balancing your energies is the reward of repairing the damage that has been done in your closest relationships and magnetizing the people who truly belong in your life. That may be an old lover, a marriage partner that you are estranged from, or a child that has not been in your life for some time. It could also be a completely new person that was meant to be in your life. When you change your energy and your perspective, everything, and everyone around you will begin to change. If it were easy to explain how to do that, I would do so in this book; however, it is a long process.

That is why it takes seven full weeks to do all the work involved. I first teach you how to balance your energy, so you recognize what it is and what it feels like. If you are doing the program properly, every day, the vibrational shift kicks in. That usually happens around the third or fourth week of doing the program. Then there is a feeling of euphoria and of being on top of the world. If you do not rebalance your energy right away, you will experience a crash, because things need to stay in balance.

Remember, for every high, there has to be a low unless you are balanced. I have taught hundreds of people the technique. Some are able to grasp all the concepts the first time through the program, and others need to do the program multiple times before they are able to balance, shift and re-balance.

It is easy to read a book, but in order to actually change your perspective you need to absorb what I teach. Everyone that completes the program is given the greatest of rewards from the Universe. Once you understand how the Universe works, and how energy works, and you can see your life from a higher perspective, your life becomes amazing. You suddenly realize that you are not here for drudgery and commonality; you are here to have an amazing life. We also are not here to be alone, work alone, or keep to ourselves.

No one is an island, and we have many people in our life that help us on many levels every day. By the same concept, we are also here to help others along their journey, in whatever capacity that entails. When you are on your life path, it all just falls into place. As you go through the program, week by week, you start to learn the five love lessons you came here to learn and can see how they have been playing out in your life.

You also have to learn that we are all here playing a role, just like an actor in a play. In order to learn your lessons, you need to not only play your role but to allow those around you to play the roles that they came here for.

For example, we reincarnate as both men and women from lifetime to lifetime. I brought through a lot of male energy when I came back this time. Not only did I take the financial lead in most of my relationships, but I was also the first person to pick up the hammer when something needed to be fixed. By doing this, I was taking away the opportunity from the male in my life to play the role that he came here for. By letting them do the "manly" things for me, hanging pictures, paying for dinner, etc., helped them learn their lessons faster.

This is just another example of how we learn the love lessons faster within a relationship.

I had a student that contacted me and came into the program after being released from prison. He was a farmer, an older, established man who had come upon some hard times, and ended up embezzling money from friends and acquaintances in the small town in which he lived. He was convicted of the crime, and his wife divorced him while he was in prison. His children disowned him, and he was shunned by everyone in his town. He was lost and on the verge of suicide when he found me.

After doing the program, and understanding why he made the choices he did, his entire life changed with the energy shift. People in the town started to come around, noticing that he was willing to talk about his situation and make an effort to pay back what he had taken. They started to have empathy and sympathy for him. They understood that sometimes we get backed into corners and make decisions we normally would not make. Then his children started to come around more and more frequently and forgave him.

He is still in love with his wife and hoping she'll come around when she is ready, but if not, he's still living his life and very happy that the lessons he learned have helped him put that chapter of his life behind him. He published a book about his experiences within a year of finishing the program and started his own business, which keeps him quite busy. His entire life has changed and is better than he thought it could ever be.

Another student of mine was a truck driver who was very despondent after losing the love of his life. He did not know how to work on a computer, and I had to teach him how to do the whole program on his cell phone. It was a little bit of a challenge for both of us since he was doing the program while working on the road, and I am not the most tech-savvy person. If someone with no computer knowledge can do the program through a cell phone, it is not that difficult.

He was committed to changing and learning the love lessons that cost him his relationship. He was not happy with his wife, and she left because she did not like the way he treated her. He only did what he learned as a child growing up and did not understand exactly what the cause of the problem was. He was not very communicative and did not really understand how to express his love and feelings. He had also never put himself first in life as he mostly worked all the time.

After completing the program, not only did he magnetize the love of his life back, but he also married her within a year. He then went on to get out of the trucking industry and started a food truck, which had been his dream. After another year, the food truck had done so well that he added a brick-and-mortar restaurant location, and he now runs the restaurant and the food truck. His life is happier and more fulfilling than he ever thought it could be since he learned his love lessons. I still hear from him quite often telling me amazing stories of how wonderful things are for both of them.

As with everything, it is always possible to slide back into your old habits. Such is the case with another student of mine. She had contacted me because she found out that her husband had been cheating on her for some time, and she was devastated. He was still living in the same house with her after she found out about the affair, and he refused to either find a new residence or lose the girlfriend. She went through the program, and not only magnetized her husband back into her life, but he also dropped the other woman and was very attentive to his wife. By making herself the focus, the dreams she always had were starting to materialize for her. He had become the attentive husband, communicating, and doing things with her as a couple the way she had always wanted.

Life was amazing for her, and then the covid shutdown hit. She fell back into all the habits she had prior to going through the program. She stopped following all the practices she had learned and went right back into her previous life. What do you think the outcome of that was for her? If you thought her husband was right back out the door, you would be correct. Not only did he cheat, but he also decided to move in with the new girlfriend and now wanted nothing to do with his wife. When the Universe gives you a gift, as it gave her with the program, and she decided to stop following it because she had gotten what she wanted, the Universe took back the reward.

You only get the reward by doing the work and continuing with what you learn. It is like the person that always wanted to buy a house. You do all the work to buy the house, and then you stop maintaining it. Eventually, it is going to fall down all around you. It will also be that much tougher to fix it once it has fallen down than if you had just maintained it while it was standing.

The program essentially works the same way. If she had continued following the love lessons she learned and meditated regularly to stay in touch with her soul, her whole life would not have just been maintained, but it would have continued to thrive. Instead, she is still struggling to magnetize him back into her life. Now the love lesson of patience will come into play because it will happen in the Universe's time, not hers. He must be learning his lessons with the other person now or teaching them something.

I offer lifetime access to the program, but she had to restart from square one and do it again from the ground up. This is a change in the way you live your life, not just something you do once and forget it. It is always your choice. It is like choosing every day to see the beauty and love that surrounds us everywhere or to look for people's faults and shortcomings. Once she restarted the program, her life again became amazing. She started traveling, reuniting with old friends, and doing things that she had stopped doing. It may take her longer for her husband to come back if that is her life plan, or she may magnetize to someone else who suits her even better.

These are the types of decisions the Universe lets us make. If you recognize that the Universe is always bringing you people and things for your highest and best, you can make an informed decision when you learn how to listen to your soul and trust it.

I had another woman, originally from England but living in New York, who was at the end of her rope with her boyfriend. They had a child together, and no matter what she said or did, not only did he refuse to marry her, but she seemed to see him less and less. He was a busy restauranteur, and although he obviously loved her, she was repelling him with her energy.

After going through the program, not only did her energy shift in a major way, but it was almost comical. As she was learning her love lessons and putting herself first, she no longer cared if he wanted to marry her, or even see her again. She started dating multiple people just to enjoy herself. The result of the program and the lessons she was learning, was her receiving not one marriage proposal, but three! It seems that not only did the two men she was dating both ask her to marry them, the one she really wanted came back with a proposal as well. She did marry him since it was what she had wanted all along, and now she is living the life she had always wanted and dreamed of. It may or may not last forever; it really depends on what she wrote into her life plan, but nonetheless, every other aspect of her life is fantastic.

I could go on and on about the students who have magnetized exactly who or what they wanted or something even better after doing the program. They have learned the majority of their love lessons by following the teachings. Some have definitely learned all the love lessons through the program and are just enjoying the lifestyle afforded us by the Universe. They marvel every day at the new and exciting things that the Universe brings their way. This is how we were meant to go through this journey called life, not in pain and suffering, but in amazement every day. We are meant to live in love and peace and wonder at all the beauty there is around us.

Final Thoughts

My hope is that everyone finds something in this book to connect to. To know that there is always hope in every day and peace in every sunset. Life is meant to be lived, not settled for, and love is the answer to every question you can ask. We all have our rollercoaster to ride, if not, life would not be as exciting and fun.

Remember to look for the rainbows, and do not be afraid to dance in the rain and take chances. Sing in the shower every chance you get, and make sure those whom you love know it and feel it. Trust that the Universe has your back, and at the end of your days, that you did the best you could do. Hopefully, through your journey, you learn your five love lessons and your life is as amazing and as much of a gift as mine has been to me.

For more information on the Relationship Mastery
Program, or to reach the author, please go to:

Free webinar: go.juneedward.com

Website address: juneedward.com

Email: june@juneedward.com

About the Author

June Edward is a psychic medium who passed to the other side during surgery at the age of 27 and came back by choice. She didn't fully embrace her gifts until later in life, and she then began working on missing person cases, as well as consulting with many well-known paranormal groups and authors.

June is an author and teacher of psychic and mediumship development and the creator of the Relationship Mastery Program, which teaches people how to change their energy, learn their five love lessons, and magnetize anyone or anything into their lives. June is credited with changing the lives of everyone who does the work and completes the program. She has mentored many people and helped to reunite hundreds of couples.